FIGHTING ENEMIES FOREIGN AND DOMESTIC

FIGHTING ENEMIES FOREIGN AND DOMESTIC

The Legacy of Angelo Codevilla

EDITED BY RYAN P. WILLIAMS

NEW YORK · LONDON

First American edition published in 2025 by Encounter Books, an activity of Encounter for Culture and Education, Inc., a nonprofit, tax-exempt corporation.
Encounter Books website address: www.encounterbooks.com

Manufactured in the United States and printed on acid-free paper. The paper used in this publication meets the minimum requirements of ANSI/NISO Z39.48—1992 (R 1997) (*Permanence of Paper*).

FIRST AMERICAN EDITION

LIBRARY OF CONGRESS CATALOGING-IN-PUBLICATION DATA IS AVAILABLE

Information for this title can be found at the Library of Congress website under the following ISBN 978-1-64177-477-2.

CONTENTS

In memory of the great and good Angelo Codevilla. May the example of his years of government service and his gift to us of decades of writing and scholarship inspire and inform his fellow patriots and statesmen in their work to save the country that he so loved.

RYAN P. WILLIAMS

INTRODUCTION

TO GET TO KNOW and spend any considerable amount of time with Angelo Codevilla was to love him. You would also argue with him – and he with you! You would almost always learn something. If you even approached being foolish or "unserious," you were not suffered gladly. Angelo was often a contentious man, and his default mode was that of instructor, sometimes patient and sometimes less so. His friends never dwelled on the last argument or correction because they knew he had equal measures of magnanimity and generosity, often poured out in small and large acts of kindness, expressions of gratitude, and world-historical hospitality.

I will not recount Angelo's biography in detail because the contributors to this volume, especially Michael Waller, do a wonderful job of giving Angelo's career its full due. Angelo was a proud naturalized citizen, a naval intelligence officer, an influential Senate staffer, a professor of international relations, a translator of Machiavelli, a senior fellow of the Claremont Institute, a longtime contributor to the *Claremont Review of Books,* and a Claremont Institute fellowship faculty member. He was a patriot, a devoted husband, and a loving father. He was also a fierce and learned critic of America's turn away from founding principles towards progressivism, especially in foreign policy.

The contributors to this volume are all students of Angelo's, whether directly or indirectly. To be a student of Angelo's was to marvel at the years of reading, thinking, interrogating, and advising that had produced the teacher. I once asked Angelo, after hours in the "hospitality suite" at a Claremont Institute fellowship program, how I could get a good education in American foreign policy according to the principles of the American Founding. "Read John Quincy Adams's diaries from 1817 to 1829, when he was Secretary of State." This was vintage Angelo: he always referred you to the source texts of the Western and American traditions and had no patience for the esteemed contemporary authorities on any given topic – even though he had invariably read most of their books, and very often skewered them in the public prints.

I'll finish with an anecdote about the first Trump administration and encourage the reader to turn the page and dig into the rest of this volume. In spring 2020, a couple of Trump-administration appointees in the Defense Department's Office of Net Assessment commissioned Angelo to write a detailed memo about what an "America First" foreign policy ought to look like. Angelo, being Angelo, a few months later delivered 70,000 words, the major theme of which was "What would John Quincy Adams do?" That very long memo, a book manuscript, really, would turn into the posthumously published 2022 book *America's Rise and Fall Among Nations: Lessons in Statecraft from John Quincy Adams*.

The story of Angelo's last book shows the man his friends working in government, policy, and ideas loved so much – and the man his adversaries loathed and feared. Angelo was advising at high levels of government but was determined to pull his audience back to the nature of things and the wisdom of great thinkers and statesmen. Committed to truth-telling whatever the venue, fiercely devoted to the recovery of the American idea, and always hard at work with a sense of urgency born of long study of, and experience with, the serious and often deadly matters of politics and statecraft, Angelo was sui generis. We all miss him dearly. His work and legacy now belong to the ages.

J. MICHAEL WALLER

THE MAN WHO KEPT THE CIA UP AT NIGHT

"ANGELO." WITH NO SURNAME NECESSARY, the mere mention put Washington's late–Cold War intelligence establishment on edge. Their tormenter was but a thirtysomething staffer on the Senate Select Committee on Intelligence. Contrarily, to the Cold Warriors sacrificing their all to defend the nation from Communist subversion and nuclear-missile threats, that single name, like a messenger from heaven, brought comfort and joy.

Angelo Codevilla knew and understood that the country that took him in as a boy would preserve itself and its founding principles by having the most capable intelligence and counterintelligence services the world had ever seen. "Most capable" didn't mean the largest, or the most lavishly funded, or supplied with the most high-tech gear. It meant having the most creative, most principled, most virtuous, and wisest people doing the job.

Angelo watched the United States' intelligence apparatus deteriorate. Visiting CIA headquarters over the years, he passed the stone inscription that the late and great CIA director Allen Dulles placed as what he intended as a permanent greeting: "And ye shall know the truth and the truth shall set you free" – the Gospel According to John. In the last year of his life, Angelo saw the videos of CIA corridors festooned with mind-numbing murals and telescreens about diversity, equity, and inclusion. To Angelo Codevilla, who spoke Latin, DEI meant "of God." A new god, a false one, possesses the American intelligence community today.

The evolution to this point was entirely predictable, and Angelo called it out early. He had the most remarkable track record of any American. Close to a half century ago on the brand-new Senate Select Committee on Intelligence, Angelo called out the CIA, not for its cult of secrecy, but for its cult of untruthfulness.

A RELENTLESS FORCE IN INTELLIGENCE OVERSIGHT

Angelo arrived in the Senate in 1977, just as George H. W. Bush left his eleven-month stint as CIA director, and as the liberal senator Frank Church wrapped up sensational hearings and reports about the intelligence community.

Angelo's committee work and intellectual rigor were so distinguished that Ronald Reagan's 1980 presidential transition team chose him to be part of its intelligence and diplomatic section. He had built a rapport with Reagan's campaign manager, the distinguished OSS veteran William J. Casey. Casey had done the unthinkable during World War II by proposing, then running, operations behind German lines after D-Day to open the invasion route for allied American, French, and British Empire forces to march to Berlin.

Rapport and mutual respect grew to deep trust when Casey ran the CIA. Angelo became Bill Casey's man in the Senate. But Angelo Codevilla was never the CIA's man. To him, the CIA was just a bureaucracy that performed a necessary function. He believed that that bureaucracy was performing its function poorly, and going in the wrong direction. No bureaucracy, he believed, was sacred. Certainly none should ever be permanent.

Angelo wasn't even Bill Casey's man. He was his own man. He stood true to his principles, never feared burning bridges, and often anticipated enjoying the flames.

Angelo trusted and admired President Reagan for the good in him, and for his ideals. He worked closely in a fraternal and trusting relationship with Reagan's national security advisor, Judge William Clark. Casey brought the Senate staffer Angelo to private White House meetings with President Reagan.

Angelo found himself in the curious situation – or, knowing him, he created that situation – of serving on the Senate committee whose job was to oversee the CIA, while also working with the CIA director himself to get ahold of the dysfunctional and demoralized bureaucracy. The CIA wasn't being truthful with Congress, and it wasn't being truthful with Casey either.

It wasn't a matter of the CIA's being secretive. Angelo had all the necessary clearances. It was a matter of being truthful. This bothered Angelo immensely. So did incompetence. And so did ideological blinders. Angelo was never in awe of the CIA or the FBI, though he did say once, thirty-three years ago, that the FBI merited some of his esteem. That was then.

That year, as the Soviet Union was collapsing, he wrote a monumental work, *Informing Statecraft: Intelligence for a New Century*, on what a successful intelligence community should look like, how it should act, and why. The CIA was far, far behind the curve, looking backward instead of forward. "The major elements of US intelligence will have to be rethought and rebuilt," he said.

Of course, they were not rethought or rebuilt until after their hand was forced – after the September 11 terror attacks. Even then, the rethinking and rebuilding was done entirely wrong. Instead of the eternal standards of philosophical soundness and professional excellence that Angelo laid out in 1991, the US intelligence system treated its bureaucratic instincts as sacrosanct, taking critical theory as its lodestar, and glowering establishmentarians cemented the new order.

The CIA leveraged its network of mid- to late-career bureaucrats – the Old Boys – to manage perceptions by leaking to the press, helping write or actually writing the popular histories, dominating the academic studies of intelligence, and credentialing those who would play well with others.

Angelo had his own exceptional network, however. He played

five-dimensional chess in his sleep. He knew all about bureaucratic warfare and subversion both as a scholar and as a practitioner. He knew exactly whom to call, when, and what to say.

Certain senators dreaded him. So did select high-ranking CIA and FBI officials.

He had a bipartisan spleen. On the Senate Intelligence Committee, Codevilla gleefully terrorized Republicans and Democrats alike with pointed, relentless inquiries that exposed intellectual inconsistencies and sheer sloppiness. He forced analysts and policymakers alike to address inconvenient facts as facts. They hated him for it, but many of them admitted he was right in private.

Angelo was known for his broad smile of iron teeth long before the Soviet foreign minister Andrei Gromyko (or a KGB officer assigned to the pliant *Washington Post* reporter Dusko Doder, who related it to the American audience) came up with the term to describe Mikhail Gorbachev.

"Iron teeth" applied to Angelo far better than it did to the Soviet leader. Codevilla's militant joviality while pummeling Washington's morally corrupt and weak-minded power elite flummoxed both friends and enemies. Hit hardest were the victims of Codevilla's intellectual inquisitions. They could never quite tell whether the iron smile was a signal of genuine joy in shepherding one lost in a sea of laziness and prejudice toward logical reasoning, or whether the smile was a precursor to a deadly verbal salvo until it was too late.

CHALLENGING THE OLD BOYS' CLUB

Angelo was a perceptive talent spotter. He sized you up quickly. He would go out of his way to help those whom he deemed earnest. He reveled in discussions of facts, reason, and philosophy. One didn't have to agree with him to be his friend. But if you were out, you were out permanently. He despised what he called "dishonest treachery."

Treachery is part of the intelligence profession. It has to be. Angelo studied treachery and respected it. Dishonest treachery, to Angelo, was treachery executed in a morally wrong way and for morally wrong reasons. The world is treacherous. People are treacherous. To navigate treachery for a cause larger than oneself, one had to understand treachery, expect it, and deal with it on its own terms.

Born in Italy during the collapse of Mussolini's fascist regime during World War II, Angelo always focused on the fundamentals. He always referenced the classics. He was the only member of the Senate Intelligence Committee staff, and perhaps the only person on earth, who read and studied the intelligence community's *entire* supersecret annual budget, line by line – a pile of papers two feet high – year after year.

Angelo had a fear-inducing way of questioning intelligence leaders. He would say, "I asked Aristotle's simple questions of officials throughout the intelligence community: What is the purpose of this activity? Why do you do this rather than something else? Do you do this for the sake of that, or vice versa? By what criteria do you judge your products good or bad?"

"I was astounded," he remarked, "at how little thought had been given to decisions that affected thousands of careers, billions of dollars, and the nation's very future. All too often the answers to my questions were 'We've always done it this way,' and 'How insulting for you to ask!'"

Angelo understood strategy the way others pretended to.

He was offending the Agency or the Bureau. Not the missions. The mission is never first in a permanent bureaucracy.

Reasoned arguments were not part of the debate. The custom, then as now, was to attack the questioner and defend the bureaucracy. Decades before DEI and LGBTQ+, the FBI had its own informal acronym for its personnel: DEB, or Don't Embarrass the Bureau.

"The attack is usually three-pronged," Angelo explained when unpacking bureaucratic argumentative tactics. "First, this person must be revealing classified information. Second, this person does not know the whole story and we who do know it are forbidden from commenting, except to say 'you're wrong.' Third, this person's demeaning tone precludes a rational explanation of some admittedly valid points."

"So, in practice, three points boil down to one: Leave the field of intelligence for the Old Boys."

The Old Boys would retire or die out, having mentored a new set of Old Boys or New Genders, or whatever the flavor of the month may be, but the goal would be the same: silence honest discussion about intelligence, counterintelligence, and whatever has become of "national security." Making truth-telling politically incorrect, and therefore wrong or immoral – and thus evil and professionally destructive – remains a defense tactic for intelligence-agency bureaucrats. Angelo decried political correctness very early as it came into vogue. As it was killed off in favor of a more virulent strain, wokeness, he continued his crusade against it.

The Old Boy networks that he called out from the 1970s became, or were already part of, what he would later define as "the Ruling Class."

WHY? WHAT FOR? AND OTHER INCONVENIENT QUESTIONS

Before the pale riders of cultural Marxism penetrated the intelligence community, Angelo was hammering away at the sheer aimlessness of American intelligence collection and analysis, most of which he saw as existing for its own sake.

After World War II and the bipartisan general consensus about containment of Communism, defining American national interests was easy: take the fight to the Communists, who were strategically mobilized to tear apart our country and our culture by any means necessary, both ideologically and physically. By defining national interests, even broadly, America could define the scope of its foreign-intelligence, counterintelligence, and national-security services.

Even the beginning faced deep flaws, plus tensions about growing globalism. That mission was poorly understood and became diluted over time, with priorities left up to "experts" from the Washington establishment and the Ivy League, further distorted by critical theorists of the Frankfurt School variety. Reagan temporarily disrupted that trend, but his monumental mission to bring down the USSR itself required immense intelligence and counterintelligence capabilities.

The end of the Soviet Union allowed anyone with eyes to see that the intelligence establishment had become, as Codevilla had warned from his Senate staff perch, a huge intelligence–industrial complex that existed more for itself than for the national interest, whatever that national interest had become.

Codevilla became one of the first serious people after the Cold War to question why the United States was pouring so many resources into technologies to spy on everything possible around the world. Surveying America's colossal human- and technological-intelligence might in 1992, he asked, "What for?"

Then, he crystallized the obvious but inconvenient facts. "To what does all of this amount? The activities to which we loosely refer as the US technical collection system was never planned according to any single purpose, nor are they administered by a single organization," he said. Some congressional oversight "sometimes prod[s] the system toward coherence. Yet coherence is elusive, because coordination is *ex post facto* to budgetary planning."

Angelo's unwelcome observation went unheeded, with Osama bin Laden proving the point with his ingeniously simple attacks of September 11, 2001, and all the Saudi and Qatari funding behind them. The al-Qaeda leader was but the most famous of a parade of "known wolves." A bright and aggressive CIA man in Sudan tried to arrange bin Laden's capture or elimination before he carried out the acts of terror he was openly planning, but he found little support up the intelligence chain, and zero at the top of the CIA and in the Clinton White House. So, bin Laden was allowed to remain free to attack.

It took a madman in a cave to force the United States to drop everything and try to add coherence to American intelligence. When that coherence came, it arrived in the hurried form of a huge centralized security apparat with near-limitless capabilities: the Office of the Director of National Intelligence, an überpowerful post which, in the wrong hands, would build coherence by abusing power and politicizing the apparat, resulting, by the time of Codevilla's death, in a largely incoherent intelligence politburo, a rogue state deeply embedded within a state, whose modus operandi became guided by a revived Comintern's critical theory and wokeness.

"Intelligence concerns human activities, and human beings, unlike God, go to great lengths to disguise their work. So perhaps the most serious charge that can be made against the fruits of US intelligence concerns not the collectors but another set of people: The counterintelligence officers who should have guarded the integrity of the collectors' work," Angelo wrote in *Informing Statecraft*. American counterintelligence failed to do so, and Codevilla is one of the very few scholars to explain why.

WEAPONIZED LANGUAGE

Angelo carefully studied language and the weaponization of words and grammar. He disdained wishy-washy intelligence products, full of caveats, euphemisms, and that terrible passive voice.

He embraced the ancient treasure of virtue. Here I speak of virtue in the Aristotelian, Hebraic, and Christian senses. Niccolò Machiavelli changed the public understanding of virtue, influencing philosophers of liberalism in subsequent centuries. He taught how to change language to trick the reader to agree with the opposite of the original definition and intent, and to reason, with easy logic, that evil was a virtue.

This was the most subversive aspect of Machiavelli's writings. Subversion is an operational part of intelligence, though seldom adequately practiced by the CIA abroad or identified and combated by the FBI to protect our constitutional republic at home (though competently waged *against* the American public). Most readers of Machiavelli rely on translations. Angelo grew frustrated with some of those translations, even those by the finest scholars. Raised in an Italian-speaking home, he read Machiavelli in its original form and discovered that, especially in the case of the Florentine's most important work, *The Prince*, the translators had "cleaned up" the Florentine evil genius's imprecise uses of words, his often poor grammar, double meaning, or doublespeak, and indeed his bad use of pronouns. The cleanups improved the flow and readability of the translations, and arguably corrected Machiavelli's sloppy mistakes.

Angelo found that Machiavelli's mistakes were purposeful, intended to convey or obscure meaning. So he set out to re-translate *The Prince*, in a literal but what he called an inelegant translation, and packed it with footnotes to explain the calculated plays on words and puns to distort language and understanding.

Machiavelli was all about power for power's sake – not for higher ideals, as Allen Dulles or Bill Casey later sought. It was simply power politics. Angelo explained how the mistranslators of Machiavelli, inadvertently or otherwise, taught people to dispense with goodness and all forms of higher purpose, to break down human relationships and society for the purposes of power. Machiavelli twisted the meaning of virtue into a "tool for wretchedness," suggesting that evil may be praiseworthy, twisting the concepts of evil and good. *The Prince*, Angelo said, marked the center of gravity from the standpoint of the sovereign: "Do I do virtuous things that don't keep me #1, or do I do evil things and stay on top?" It refers to no higher purpose than that.

And so Angelo foresaw, whether translating Machiavelli or writing on – and acting for – intelligence, counterintelligence, and national security, that the machinery created to defend our constitutional republic has been perverted to seek and preserve power for power's sake. The CIA as a bureaucracy, the FBI as a bureaucracy, Old Boy networks against citizens, the Ruling Class, political correctness, wokeness, critical theory, and cultural Marxism are all effectively automatons stockpiling power for their own sake.

SUBVERSION

Treachery had a love child called subversion. Few mainstream American studies of intelligence or counterintelligence over the past six decades or so devote much attention to subversion – how both to defend ourselves and our society against it, and to utilize it against our enemies. Codevilla treated subversion as a natural human behavior. He devoted a whole chapter to it in *Informing Statecraft*.

He also made a study of one of the 20th century's most notorious subversives, the Italian Comintern man Antonio Gramsci. Gramsci took the gradualist, cultural-Marxist approach to revolution, combining the evils of Marxism with the evils of Machiavelli and a dash of Mussolini to give us an early strain of critical theory.

Few besides Gramsci knew and applied Machiavelli as well as Angelo. Gramsci did it to subvert and destroy Western civilization. Codevilla understood and explained Machiavelli in a bid to save civilization and its moral foundations, and to save its chief protector, at least then: the United States of America.

Angelo also understood Gramsci's kindred spirits at the Germany-based Frankfurt School, also a Comintern enterprise, which rooted at Columbia University and fanned out through the Ivy League and West Coast universities. The Frankfurt School populated the OSS Research and Analysis Branch during World

War II, infiltrated the early CIA's intelligence directorate and its analytical products with a cultural-Marxist worldview, and penetrated the FBI after Robert Mueller's centralization and indiscriminate mass hires following 9/11, which is quite likely why President Obama asked Congress to extend Mueller's statutory ten-year term limit as director for another two years, making the then cognitively impaired Mueller the second-longest-reigning FBI director since J. Edgar Hoover. This wreaked damage that the rest of us are only beginning to understand as we see the rot of critical theory permeate the intelligence community, just as it has our military and educational systems.

Angelo called it early. In a work on political warfare that he wrote in 2006 titled *Political Warfare: Means for Achieving Political Ends*, he noted that, as dangerous as the enemy spies are who steal secrets, they merely steal secrets. Alger Hiss was a valuable Soviet spy, but his greatest value to the Soviet enemy was something else by far: a major controlled agent of influence and recruiter for Moscow within the Democrat and diplomatic establishments.

Worse than the spies who steal secrets and the controlled agents of influence, Angelo warned, were the subversive, uncontrolled fellow travelers, the so-called innocents and useful idiots who followed and mainstreamed the work of controlled agents – the men who designed the sellout to Stalin at Yalta, for example.

Since World War II, United States foreign policy succeeded despite, not because of, its giant intelligence–industrial apparat, Codevilla argued in his 1992 book. *Informing Statecraft* is so fundamental, and its principles and guidance so timeless, that it remains among the most important and informative volumes on both statecraft and intelligence more than three decades later. A future president should require all his intelligence, national-security, and foreign-policy appointees to master the book.

American intelligence and counterintelligence understand little of this in terms of performing their missions that the public has entrusted to them. Nor does Congress, which makes the laws.

Nor do the courts which interpret them. Nor do all but a very few of the nation's schools. And so Angelo Codevilla's approach to intelligence laid the foundations for his studies of America's national character and of the Ruling Class.

ENDURING CHARACTER

To Angelo, America's superpower status was an exception to its exceptionalism, an anomaly brought about by its defeat of fascism and its brief but squandered winning of the Cold War over the Soviet Union and Communism. The post-Soviet world, he reasoned, was time for America to return to its founding roots.

Nations have character. Their governments affect society, the moral order, and family. In a vicious circle, politics make or break all. The Founding Fathers of the United States were all men of character. They spoke openly of virtue, not in the twisted Machiavellian sense, but in its real essence.

A coherent and strategic foreign policy was a core element of the American Revolution, the founding of the American constitutional republic, and the growth of the United States and the American dream to become a superpower. The greatest successes occurred when American intelligence, like the federal government itself, was very limited and very small, and when US strategic goals were simple and understandable to the average citizen who could support them.

Times are different, but the principle remains. The United States needs a strong foreign secret-intelligence service to collect and analyze information on issues vital to its national interests to inform a president and his administration. It needs a similar service to conduct activities covertly that diplomats and the military cannot or should not do. It needs a robust counterintelligence service to neutralize foreign spying and influence against us, and a moderate security service to defend against violent or subversive internal threats to the Constitution.

Sheer size bears no relation to strength and robustness. As the world's sole superpower, the United States built a Leviathan government that created a new Ruling Class through a form of bureaucracy and corporatism that linked political power and wealth. It attacked family, religious belief, and personal character. Surveying history, and stressing the profound America chronicled by Alexis de Tocqueville, Angelo in 1997 recognized the culture wars underway that ultimately begat today's critical theory of wokeness.

How could America keep the peace in the world if it wasn't even at peace with itself? Angelo naturally wrote a book about it: *To Make and Keep Peace*, subtitled *Among Ourselves and with All Nations*. Much earlier, with Paul Seabury, he wrote one of the most important modern textbooks of peace's opposite, titled *War: Ends and Means*. And then, he provided a collection of essays during the Global War on Terrorism, titled *No Victory, No Peace*, which observed, in what would mark the early part of a forever war, "The Bush Administration has not achieved peace because it has not sought victory." That was back in 2005.

Angelo constantly asked the annoying question, "Why go to war if you don't intend to win?"

A common thread bound all his works on conflict, defense, intelligence, peace, and treachery. That thread was about keeping America first, a solid and reasoned approach without the politicized jingoism, and tempered by a firm grounding in American founding principles and the Western moral tradition.

As time went by, after Reagan's successful strategy brought down the Soviet Union and the military–industrial and intelligence–industrial complexes mushroomed to what they are today, Angelo focused extensively on the elites who run American politics and policy, and the uniparty that became known as the Swamp and the permanent Ruling Class.

As an aside, perhaps Angelo's most impactful legacy, more than forty years ago, was to build up a leader in the US Senate to push for a space-based weapons system to shoot down incoming ballistic nuclear missiles. This effort involved constant coordination with the Reagan White House. A Soviet active-measures campaign aimed at weak and treacherous politicians and other elites kept Congress from providing the funds to build and deploy that revolutionary, workable system. The prospect of an American strategic missile-defense system wrecked the Soviets' nuclear war calculus and, with Reagan's own nuclear modernization, tricked the Kremlin into bankrupting the USSR with needless new weapons programs that Reagan planned to negotiate away. However, Congress never funded a functional space-based missile defense and, to this day, America remains completely vulnerable to a strategic nuclear-missile attack.

The Ruling Class, as personified by President George W. Bush and Hillary Rodham Clinton, never tried to understand the nature of the jihadist enemy. Angelo called them out for it at the time. Unlike in domestic politics, where they worked tirelessly to keep themselves in power, he observed, they never sought to win abroad. The same was true for the permanent class within the military and intelligence communities. Indeed, by the 2000s, the Joint Chiefs of Staff had completely removed the word "victory" from its annual four-hundred-page *Dictionary of Military and Associated Terms*.

On learning this during dinner with friends, Angelo grew incensed but was not at all surprised, switching the conversation to pose the question, "Why have a military if our leaders say nothing of victory?"

This need for an endlessly growing spy machine resulted more through the incrementalism of American interventionism and forever wars than through a grand design for a giant foreign and domestic spy apparat, or so we'd like to think, but the result was the same. A grandly designed spy apparat would have been more logical and effective than the one we have.

Angelo Codevilla flew with the high and mighty, not because he craved being among them but because he knew he had to be.

Even in Washington, he always took the time to mentor young people to become the next generation of diplomats, spies, and national-security leaders.

He taught, among remarkable colleagues, at Boston University during the years when the BU president John Silber was on the cusp of transforming the middling school into a top-flight institution with a world-class national-security and international-diplomacy program – a transformation that died with Silber and swirled down the loo of intellectual mediocrity, wokeness, and the scam of critical-race-theory corruption. Still, Boston University's very woke Pardee School of Global Studies, of which Angelo was never on the faculty because the school didn't exist at the time, proudly claims him as a professor emeritus.

MERE BUREAUCRACIES IN NEED OF REPLACEMENT

Government bureaucracies are just bureaucracies. When they atrophy and abuse the public trust, they should be abolished. In an orderly way, their essential functions can be transferred to another bureaucracy that can do the job, or, better yet, they can be culled to create a new bureaucracy to last for as long as it faithfully executes its intended purpose.

Angelo agreed that we don't need the FBI and CIA as they are. But that *doesn't* mean that America doesn't need strong foreign-intelligence, counterintelligence, and even internal-security agencies to defend the country and its interests from foreign adversaries. Bureaucracies come and go. And just as the FBI and the CIA came at parts of the distant past, Angelo argued in his later years that it was time for them to go in favor of something better.

Replacements would have to be designed according to the priorities of America's mission in the world, which he saw as driven by the American people's priorities for the central government to serve them, with their consent as the governed, and not for the Ruling Class to serve itself. The people determine their needs, the elected officials determine strategies and policies to fulfill those needs, and then the officials design and authorize the intelligence apparatus necessary to execute those strategies and policies.

And this is where Angelo labored his last. For years he had referred to the America seen by Tocqueville – its mission, its place in the world, its relations with foreign countries, and its securing its own defense. His last work, published posthumously in 2022, drew lessons in statecraft from an intellectual and political giant and near-forgotten contemporary of Tocqueville, President John Quincy Adams.

Although America had leading political families such as the Adamses even when Tocqueville made his observations, there was no Ruling Class. America's founders fought relentlessly to avoid the emergence of a national class of elites, even though several states in the federation had their own dominant political or economic families and clans. But there was no massive, permanent central government with a constellation of companies with business models of milking the taxpayers' udders. There was no interstate Ruling Class.

The superficiality of popular American history almost passes over John Quincy Adams, viewing him as the son of a Founding Father and a one-term president during a period of undistinguished one-termers.

In *America's Rise and Fall Among Nations: Lessons in Statecraft from John Quincy Adams*, Codevilla described a true American foreign policy, one as consistent with the vision of the Founding Fathers as with present-day America First nationalism. Adams was the brilliant but practically forgotten 19th-century secretary of state and president who, as a five-year-old, had been brought by his parents, John and Abigail Adams, to watch the Battle of Bunker Hill in 1775.

John Quincy Adams effectively founded US foreign policy and grand strategy. He authored the Monroe Doctrine to preserve the independence of the new American republics from Mexico to South America, and to keep European powers out of the region.

In studying Adams's extraordinary experiences as diplomat, secretary of state, president, and statesman, Codevilla showed America's successes in determining its own national interests in geopolitics by limiting them, reducing the need for a global, expeditionary military and a centralized, European-style security state to prop up, among other things, a Ruling Class. He celebrated John Quincy Adams's principles and achievements – among them, ghostwriting the extraordinarily successful Monroe Doctrine as secretary of state – and tracked American foreign policy and geostrategy from Adams's time to the present, uncovering a consistency of principles regardless of international circumstances.

Application of those principles is directly associated with America's rise. Abandonment of them, over time, tracks with America's relative decline. Revival of them, Codevilla would argue, would be cause for optimism.

ROBERT REILLY

ANGELO CODEVILLA, THE ANTI-MILLENARIAN

THE 20TH-CENTURY COMPOSER Igor Stravinsky remarked on how much he disliked the music of his contemporary Richard Strauss. A music critic asked, "Maestro, could you be more specific?" Stravinsky answered, "Yes. I do not like the major works, and I do not like the minor works."

Angelo Codevilla was above all an anti-millenarian. If asked to be more specific, he would have answered, "Yes. I do not like millenarianism in domestic policy, and I do not like millenarianism in foreign policy." In one fell swoop, Angelo was "Fighting Enemies Foreign and Domestic," both of whom suffered from the same symptom – the inability to recognize limits.

Millenarianism was not a subject that Angelo often addressed directly, though he did so in the Summer 2020 *Claremont Review of Books*, in an essay titled "Millenarian Mobs." There are many significant points in Angelo's work, far too many to examine in a chapter, but the most significant is the foundation from which he set his course. This is not often commented upon because, most of the time, Angelo was criticizing misconceived foreign and domestic policies in meticulous detail or skewering the Ruling Class – all the while doing so with his signature incisiveness of thought and clarity of expression.

The two main sources of his anti-millenarian orientation derived from his depth of learning in the Greek classics, especially Aristotle and Plato, and from his profound Christian faith, which he always took as compatible with reason. We often discussed our mutual love of Norman Cohn's classic *The Pursuit of the Millennium: Revolutionary Millenarians and Mystical Anarchists of the Middle Ages*, along with Hans Jonas's *The Gnostic Religion*. These works, and those of Eric Voegelin and Leo Strauss, had a large impact on those of us who were seeking to understand the spiritual sickness underlying modern totalitarian ideology. Angelo particularly benefited from his studies with Gerhart Niemeyer at Notre Dame and Harry V. Jaffa at Claremont Graduate School.

Anti-millenarianism provided Angelo's anchoring orientation. He was a metaphysical realist, grounded in *what is*, or *ta onta*, as Socrates called it – Greek words Angelo was fond of quoting. This is the grounding from which he gained his deep understanding of, and allegiance to, natural law, which gives direction to the ends inherent in things, as well as to the limits naturally abiding in them: in other words, the order of nature. It is, after all, the nature of things that both makes them possible and limits their possibilities. It is this perspective that led Angelo to challenge the progressives for their unnatural understanding of the pliability of reality, most especially reflected in the limitlessness of their objectives. They think they can change reality by willing it so.

Within the realist order, how is man to understand himself? The answer requires the broadest perspective within which man finds meaning. As Angelo knew, Judeo-Christian tradition shaped the West by assigning evil's origin to Original Sin – a cataclysmic dislocation in the relationship between God and man that resulted in "fallen nature." The essence of that sin is a disorder within man himself, the preference of oneself to God: pride. Salvation, the restoration of the proper God–man relationship, could only be achieved by the sacrifice of Christ and then by man's renouncing evil with good works in cooperation with God's grace. The good man finds his fulfillment when uniting with God in the afterlife. The Christian view was thus comprehensive: it explained man's origins in God's creation, the existence of evil from Original Sin, and the final triumph of salvation in Christ over evil and death.

Life was understandable in these terms: it had a meaning and purpose with which man could transform his sufferings into something endurable and ultimately salvific. If man could not feel at home here, he had the reassurance that he was meant for elsewhere. "Thou hast made us for Thyself, Oh Lord, and our hearts are restless until they rest in Thee," wrote St. Augustine in his *Confessions*.

Man's end, then, was *outside* of history in personal union with a transcendent and loving God. The great Christian contribution to the question of man's nature and his ultimate end is the revelation that man's soul is not only drawn to the good but to goodness itself, which is God. His true home is not the polis, but the City of God, in which he will truly become God-like. Socrates' "city in speech" finds its true location and reality in Augustine's *City of God*.

Christianity removed from the political order any pretension to fulfill man's highest end through its own means. Ironically, in offering a vision that transcends politics, Christianity saved politics from itself or, rather, from trying to be something other than itself, by enabling it to focus on its proper realm: how best to govern man in the temporal world by so arranging the things of this life that he can peacefully pursue his transcendent end, achieving in this realm what Augustine called *tranquillitas ordinis* – "tranquility of order," or peace – the highest end of which politics is capable.

A practical expression of this perspective is in the US Constitution, an anti-millenarian document if there ever was one. It implicitly acknowledges Original Sin and its baneful effects in that it does not offer any solution to the problem of evil. The notion of Original Sin discourages government from undertaking something of which it is incapable. The Founding Fathers clearly considered a solution to evil beyond the realm of politics and their own individual competences, which is why they *necessarily* limited government. Angelo noted that the founders thought a solution to evil existed, even if the Constitution did not provide one. "Indeed, they believed that the 'solution,' in the form of Christianity, was so widely known and accepted by them and their fellow countrymen that there was no need to make it explicit," wrote Angelo.

Limited government does not – and due to its limited nature cannot – usurp man's destiny or grant itself salvific aims. It implicitly acknowledges the need for salvation and its own impotence before this need. Politics cannot meet the needs of the human soul, for it cannot achieve perfect justice.

The founders realized that one must look beyond politics for spiritual fulfillment. Socrates showed that any attempt to fulfill the soul's ultimate desire through politics, by trying to achieve perfect justice on Earth, would transform the state into a totalitarian enterprise. The founders knew this. Without this limiting view of politics, constitutional thinking would not have been possible. Only a vision like this supports the effort to restrain political power. It is also this view that should restrain any impulses to democratic millenarianism.

What happens when the political order transgresses its own ends and confuses itself with a metaphysical project beyond its scope – as in transforming the nature of reality through power, instantiating a brave new world, transgressing the inviolable line between the transcendent and the terrestrial? Christianity is the staunchest guardian against the ever-present temptation for politics to displace the spiritual order and take upon itself man's salvation. In *Truth and Tolerance*, Cardinal Joseph Ratzinger warned, "Wherever politics tries to be redemptive, it is promising too much. Where it wishes to do the work of God, it becomes not divine, but demonic." The horrors of Nazi Germany, the Soviet Union, and Communist China, regimes that attempted to eliminate Christianity to clear the way for their own efforts at man's self-deification, substantiate this claim. As we said along with Angelo, this is the result of transgressing the border between the terrestrial and the transcendent. Angelo's allegiance to *ta onta* and his Christian faith underlay both his intellectual and practical efforts to oppose these efforts. He wrote, "Judeo-Christianity teaches that perfection is not of this world."

Eric Voegelin called these ideologies the "stop-history" systems that dominated the twentieth century. He averred that they can "maintain the appearance of truth only by an act of violence, i.e., by prohibiting questions concerning the premises and by making the prohibition a formal part of the system. This interdict on the question is the symptom of a self-contradiction which makes the existentially open participation in the process of reality impossible."

Karl Marx offered a perfect example of a "stop-history" system when he forbade his followers from even thinking upon the matter of contingency because there cannot be an infinite regression of contingent, caused beings. There must be an uncaused cause (God) to begin a chain of contingent beings. Therefore, announced Marx, "this question is forbidden socialist man."

At its heart, ideology is a search for a substitute divinity in man himself, a "New Man" who can then establish his version of heaven on earth. Karl Marx said, "The religion of the workers has no God, because it seeks to restore the divinity of man." Man could save himself by becoming something other than human. Alain Besançon calls ideology "a doctrine that, in exchange for conversion, promises a temporal salvation that claims to conform to a cosmic order whose evolution has been scientifically deciphered and requires a political practice aimed at radically transforming society." The result, invariably, is tyranny.

Back in the 1970s, a humorously meant motto, playing off Eric Voegelin's sometimes abstruse language, was "Don't let them immanentize the eschaton." The quip does, however, capture for those who understand its terms the essence of millenarianism. The dictionary definition of eschaton is "the consummation of history, including the Last Judgment and the defeat of evil, the eternal blessedness of the righteous, and, in some traditions, the creation of a new heaven and earth." Let us briefly take a look at the nature of modern ideology as a terrestrial replacement. The term "ideology" as used here does not mean, of course, just any group of ideas, but rather a comprehensive set of ideas set against reality as a replacement for it, forging an ostensibly coherent system of thought. Socrates said that the worst thing we can have in our souls is a lie about *what is*. For Angelo, modern ideology was such a lie, a denial of reality that could only be disastrous. Its hallmark is how dismissive it is of reality. It is always reductive and deformative in its war on reality, all the while seeming to build a brave new edifice, which invariably crumbles due to its lack of foundation in reality.

To import forcefully into time what properly belongs outside of time is a clear example of the most radical progressivism, which takes modern science as its principal instrument. After all, what is it that modern science recognizes it cannot do? Science replaces faith as the arbiter of ultimate things at the price of "immanentizing the eschaton," absorbing into the political realm projects that do not belong in it at the price of distorting political ends and losing theological moorings that safeguard mankind in its ultimate meaning and destiny. To relocate the eschatological realm, Communism and Nazism appropriated transcendent goals with the claim that they are all achievable in the here and now. Those opposing such projects are, as President Obama said, on the "wrong side of history."

The prototypical totalitarianism of the French Revolution demonstrated what happens when the border between the terrestrial and transcendent is transgressed. "Now as ever," wrote Angelo, "they are about destroying civilization in the name of altering the human condition. From the time of the French Revolution until today, human beings have experienced [this] as violent, revolutionary totalitarianism."

It is worth seeing how "total" totalitarianism is by examining the French Revolution in detail, as I endeavored to do in chapter 10 of *America on Trial*, from which most of what comes below is taken. In *The Progress of the Human Mind*, the Marquis de Condorcet epitomized the French Enlightenment's ambition: "The results of my work will be to show from reasoning and from facts, that no bounds have been fixed to the improvement of the human faculties, that *the perfectibility of man is absolutely indefinite*" (emphasis added). In fact, this endeavor might involve extending man's life with "no assignable limits." Man's perfectible future "has no other limit than the duration of the globe on which nature has placed us," Condorcet wrote. He went on to argue that the state provides the vehicle for organizing and implementing man's self-perfection. Here are some of the details of what followed.

The transformation of mankind and the conquest of death are not political goals, but metaphysical ones: to remove man from contingency, to restart if not to end history, to make man completely at home in the world by transforming him into God and his world into paradise through the total subversion of, and total revolution against, reality as it is: the end of *ta onta*. This enterprise would place within man's hands the complete means to his own happiness. Man's aspiration for the divine is actually for something already within *himself* that only needs to be unlocked to be realized. The French Revolution was key to this undertaking. *Ex nihilo* and *de novo*, it was based on the assumption that, as Eric Voegelin characterized it, "a change in the order of being lies in the realm of human action, that this salvational act is possible through man's own effort." This is what the claim to unlimitedness means. The British statesman Edmund Burke knew what it foreshadowed: "In the groves of their academy, at the end of every vista, you see nothing but the gallows."

If Condorcet was the metaphysician of this movement, the Marquis de Sade was its theologian, or rather its anti-theologian. Sade was liberated from his confinement for rape and other outrages by the revolution. He was promoted to a government commission, though he was later incarcerated again, this time by Robespierre. (The newly minted "Citizen Sade" was not the only released pornographer to play a role; Mirabeau, author of *Erotika Biblion* and *Ma Conversion, ou le libertin de qualité*, became a major figure in the Assembly.) In *The Philosophy of the Boudoir*,

Sade wrote that the murder of King Louis XVI was insufficient to bring about the desired revolutionary freedom. The morality of the social and political order had survived the king's beheading. How could it finally be destroyed? In the first known use of the phrase, Sade wrote that the murder of the king must be followed by the "murder of God." As he said, "the idea of God is the sole wrong for which I cannot forgive mankind."

Louis Saint-Just, one of the key figures of the Reign of Terror and a member of the Committee of Public Safety, was a close colleague of Maximilien Robespierre, to whom he had written by way of introduction: "You whom I know only, as I know God, by his miracles." Saint-Just was a radical ideologue for whom the achievement of a perfect society justified the elimination of all opposition. He said, "What makes a Republic is the total destruction of whatever stands in its way." This included Louis XVI, whose execution Saint-Just eloquently advocated. He declared that "a government has for principle either virtue or Terror. What do they want, who want neither virtue nor Terror?" and that "nothing so resembles virtue as a great crime."

Murder in the name of virtue became the prototype for subsequent totalitarian revolutions and regimes. In another preview of totalitarianism, Saint-Just predicted: "It is in the nature of things for our economic affairs to become more and more embroiled until the Republic, once established, takes over all operations, all interests, all rights, all obligations, and imposes a common pattern on all parts of the State." Power is to reside in the laws "which take the place of God." Dubbed by later writers as the "Angel of Death," he was overheard to say that "A nation can regenerate itself only upon mounds of corpses." He proclaimed, "We must not only punish traitors, but all people who are not enthusiastic. There are only two kinds of citizens: the good and the bad. The Republic owes to the good its protection. To the bad it owes only death." Thus, he advised the Convention: "The vessel of the Revolution can arrive in port only on a sea reddened with torrents of blood." A close confidant of Robespierre, he went to his death by guillotine with his mentor on July 28, 1794.

During the short span from September 5, 1793, to July 27, 1794, some 300,000 French suspects were arrested and tens of thousands were executed or died in prison. More victims fell in the Vendée after the brutal suppression of the peasant uprising there, including the execution of hundreds of children.

The French Revolution attempted a total break with the past by destroying it. It dated the inception of the French Republic as the year "zero." It adopted a calendar to begin time anew with 1793 as the first year of the new era, restarting history, this time without God's providence. Sundays were eliminated as part of the dechristianization campaign that instituted a new ten-day week. Christianity had to be eliminated because it anchored man's destiny in the afterlife and was inimical to all the revolution's pretensions.

In 1793, the French revolutionaries transformed Notre-Dame into the Temple of Reason, where they constructed a huge mound of earth on which they enthroned the Goddess of Liberty, a voluptuous opera singer. One of the key coordinators of the event, Jacques Hébert, reported, "What a spectacle to see all the children of liberty rushing into the former cathedral to purify the temple of all the absurdity and to dedicate it to truth and reason!" An altar to Truth supported effigies of Voltaire and Rousseau, among others. The organizer of the event, Pierre-Gaspard Chaumette, was so ashamed of his Christian name that he changed it to Anaxagoras because of the latter's alleged atheism for which he was indicted in 5th-century BC Athens. Condorcet celebrated that "The abasement of reason before the delirium of a supernatural faith disappeared from society, as it has disappeared from philosophy." Citizen Sade told the Convention that "Reason is replacing Mary in our temples and the incense that used to burn at the knees of an adulterous woman will from now on be kindled only at the feet of the goddess who broke our chains."

Churches were closed or converted into temples of reason,

their bells melted down for bullets or coinage. Christian symbols were removed. Crosses were taken from graveyards. The anthropocentric Cult of Reason reigned. Under it, there would be, according to Anacharsis Cloots, "one God only, *Le Peuple*." In his address to the National Convention (November 17, 1793), Cloots proclaimed: "Citizens, religion is the greatest obstacle to my utopia." The dechristianization campaign led to persecution of Christians and, in some cases, the killing of clergy. Some 25,000 priests tried to flee the country. They didn't all make it. On September 2, 1792, writes E. Michael Jones, "wagons carrying 115 defenseless priests bound for deportation were diverted by an enraged mob to the Abbaye and a Carmelite convent." As Citizen Sade reported, "all of the refractory priests had their throats cut in the churches where they were being held, among them the Archbishop of Arles, the most virtuous and respectable of men." One of the most infamous episodes during the Terror was the execution of the Carmelite sisters of Compiègne. Declared enemies of the state for secretly practicing their vows, the sixteen sisters were marched to the scaffold and guillotined on July 17, 1794. Voltaire had said, "Every sensible man, every honorable man must hold the Christian religion in horror." Therefore, he famously urged, "crush the infamous," and they did.

Anyone well-versed in Angelo's teachings would have no trouble in diagnosing what lay behind these horrific disorders, with more to come. From the evils of the French Revolution it was but a short jump to its descendant, the Russian Revolution, and from there to the Frankfurt School and Herbert Marcuse, whose malign influence has penetrated into the American elite. Angelo was right in calling the elite of the United States – the Ruling Class – corrupt. It was their embrace of the progressivist heresy that made them so. Angelo recalled that "politically correct" is a Communist expression and noted with some amusement that "The notion of political correctness came into use among Communists in the 1930s as a semi-humorous reminder that the Party's interest is to be treated as a reality that ranks above reality itself." An old joke runs, "Comrade, your statement is factually incorrect." To which the Comrade responds: "Yes, it is. But it is politically correct." So might say a modern American progressivist.

Angelo was prudent in his application of principles to circumstances. This prudence undergirded his admiration for John Quincy Adams, the quintessential prudent man and leader. "Along with Adams," Angelo said, "I see new modes and orders as not so likely to improve human character as they are to worsen it." He certainly shared Augustine's pessimism over what was possible politically because of man's fallen nature and his belief that the best of what can be hoped for is *tranquillitas ordinis*. Fighting a war always is or should be about winning the peace. Not for Angelo the word "crusade," which connoted an intemperance and inability to recognize the limits of what was possible.

Regrettably, millenarianism was not limited to left-wing progressives. Angelo was dumbfounded at the millenarianism in President George W. Bush's second inaugural address, announcing an impossible "ultimate goal of ending tyranny in our world." "Just three days removed from these events," the president said, shortly after 9/11, "Americans do not yet have the distance of history. But our responsibility to history is already clear: to answer these attacks and *rid the world of evil*" (emphasis added), a millenarian ambition if ever there was one. Bush said, "We are led, by events and common sense, to one conclusion: The survival of liberty in our land increasingly depends on the success of liberty in other lands. The best hope for peace in our world is the expansion of freedom in all the world." This has been nowhere and at no time "common sense." The limitlessness of Bush's goals shows that millenarianism can infect both sides of the aisle. On November 18, 2023, President Biden followed in Bush's footsteps, declaring in a *Washington Post* op-ed, "Our goal should not be simply to stop the war for today – it should be to end the war forever, break the cycle of unceasing violence."

But Bush and Biden did not invent American political millenarianism. Angelo noted that the credit belongs to President

Woodrow Wilson. Wilson was the progenitor in expressing this limitless objective, while providing its underlying principle: "The interests of all nations are our own." Angelo wrote that "the Progressives' paramount premise is precisely that US policy's proper primary concern must be with mankind as a whole, and with America only incidentally and derivatively." Wilson rejected traditional American statesmanship, which focused on the interests of the United States as its first and primary duty.

Angelo saw that America's endless wars were usually the effect of the inability to "mind our own business." The underlying cause was in the failure to understand exactly what is America's business. Get that wrong, and even a successful military operation would be futile. Afghanistan and Iraq serve as examples. The United States could absorb the blows of its failures, but only if it learned its lessons. In that we failed, as became evident in the Afghanistan fiasco. Millenarianism prevailed because it was embedded in the mission. Angelo thought the initial strike against the Taliban was not only justified, but necessary. After the Taliban's destruction, he thought we should have left after turning things over to the Northern Alliance. We did the opposite by disarming the Northern Alliance and attempting to install a centralized government, just what Afghans have never accepted, and to liberate their women. The cultural renovation of the Afghan people to make them suitable for modern constitutional government was a goal formed by either ignorance or hubris. Perhaps the iconic image of American incomprehension of Afghan culture was the LGBTQ+ flag flying at the US embassy in Kabul. Angelo's standard for success in war could serve as the obituary for America's failure in Afghanistan: "The test of military operations is whether, if and when they are successful at killing the people intended to be killed, the troubles persist or not. If the troubles do persist, it means ... that the people who were killed were less troublesome than those left alive, and hence that the military operations were ill conceived."

In spite of his disdain for military misadventures, Angelo had a deep appreciation of the nature of the threats to the United States from ideological regimes whose universal ambitions were spawned by their missions to remake reality. Reality, after all, is everywhere. It was only prudent to oppose such regimes with vigor since one's own elimination was the sine qua non for the success of, say, the Nazi regime or of the Soviet Union before and after it. Angelo was not only a theorist but a practical man who fought against such overweening ideological projects whether undertaken by enemies of the United States overseas or by the radical progressivists at home. Angelo's service as a naval intelligence officer demonstrated his commitment at the practical level to meeting such threats. However, far more valuable was his theoretical knowledge from his deep study of the Marxist-Leninist ideology propelling the Soviet Union.

Within the conduct of war, Angelo had a keen appreciation for the role of the war of ideas. War's practical objective, he said, is to cause the enemy to give up the ideas that animate his struggle, either by demonstrating the illegitimacy of his ideas or crushing those who hold them – or more likely a combination of the two. It also serves to convince the enemy that further pursuit of his ideas is futile, or just no longer worth the effort. "Willingness to kill and die signifies seriousness," wrote Angelo. Yet the key to victory in the war of ideas is "which side proves that it represents something worth killing and dying for?" It would be nice to have comparable metrics to measure whether or not one is succeeding in the war in men's minds. We can map geographic territory; we can even map cultural terrain. It is nigh impossible to map the human soul. It has intangibles that are not quantifiable. Its movements have no ready metrics. As Ayatollah Khomeini famously said, "the revolution is not about the price of melons." Ideas are not commodities. Try to measure them as if they were, and you miss their essence. Yet how, and in what way, or in which direction ideas move is decisive for the outcome.

How, then, can you tell if you are winning the war of ideas? The answer, said Angelo, is by the language people use, by the way in which they express what is right or what is "good," by the way they define what is legitimate and what is not. Angelo said that ultimate victory comes when the enemy speaks your language and embraces your idea of the right, if he accepts your standard of justice and concedes the legitimacy of your cause. This means not simply the same words, but the same *meaning* of those words. Victory, so defined, may have to come from military defeat, as it did for the Japanese in World War II. So much the better that the Soviet Union collapsed peacefully because it lost its legitimacy in the eyes of its own people.

Angelo's legacy then is that of practical realism, buttressed by metaphysical realism. He had probed deeply into the Marxist-Leninist heresy and its descendants. Equally he had delved into the fantasy of Wilsonian idealism and its dangerous, all-too-real consequences for American society. In both cases he cautioned his countrymen to tread carefully but courageously, holding tightly to reason and its Judeo-Christian inheritance in an uncertain future.

DAVID CORBIN

ANGELO CODEVILLA'S AMERICA

"A POSSESSION FOR ALL TIME"

> *Thucydides, an Athenian, wrote the history of the war between the Peloponnesians and the Athenians, beginning at the moment that it broke out, and believing that it would be a great war, and more worthy of relation than any that had preceded it. This belief was not without its grounds.*
>
> THUCYDIDES, *History of the Peloponnesian War*, 1.1

THE WAR BETWEEN the Peloponnesians and the Athenians would, in time, be the undoing of both the Spartan and Athenian regimes and lead to the demise of the Greek city-state that had galvanized the 5th-century BC Hellenic world.

In the 21st century, the American republic finds itself in a similarly imperiled, perhaps irrecoverable, position. As the regime is rightly regarded as the best hope for ordered liberty in the modern world, it is unsurprisingly at the center of a civilizational civil war that threatens to tear the West apart.

A naturalized citizen, Angelo Codevilla believed the American experiment in self-government representative of modern republicanism at its best, and worthy of reverence and preservation. His effort to show how America evolved from the founding to the present day in its domestic and foreign affairs was shaped by the same purpose that moved the likes of Thucydides – that in capturing America's "rise and fall among nations" he might convey to posterity a "possession for all time."

Though he labored for the American republic established by

the founders, Codevilla's endeavor did not amount to offering a set of political prescriptions as to how it might be recovered. In fact, near the end of his career, he posited that America had moved beyond its republican moorings. What, then, was to be done? If the American republic, like all of history's most excellent regimes, is actualized only for a moment in time, Codevilla's works and writings suggest that its survival is possible in the form of communicable understanding as transmitted with piercing clarity, resolution, and devotion.

He shared this understanding more with the tone and aspect of a patriarch counseling his sons. While this type of education is hard, involves pointed admonishment and exhortation, and is difficult to impart at the macro-political level, it represents the best means of understanding the extent and limits of political excellence given the ways of the world. And we would do well to understand his thoughts on how we arrived at this point to better move forward in our troubled times. This essay proceeds on the assumption, as Codevilla oft expressed, that the statesman's first responsibility, like the physician dealing with a sick patient, is "first, to do no harm." Thereafter, the statesman must mark out the best possible outcome – defined in terms of his nation's desired peace and circumscribed by its political and material resources – and, using the available tools at his disposal, work toward that end.

SETTING THE STAGE: REINTRODUCING THE CONCEPT OF REGIME

Codevilla explained in his preface to *The Character of Nations* (1997) that his arrival in America as an Italian immigrant and early student of classical political thought introduced him to how regimes shape the character of political communities.

> As an adolescent Italian learning to be an American in the 1950s, I gained a painful glimpse into the possibilities for

> change in human beings. The Greek classics taught me that habit and circumstance make for very different ways of life. Plato and Aristotle's descriptions of how Lycurgus's laws made the Spartans dogged while Solon's laws made the Athenians expansive made sense. So did Thucydides' account of the Macedonian barbarians adopting Greek ways while any number of Greeks were degenerating into barbarism. And what was Roman history if not the tale of human character and political institutions rising and falling intertwined? As I devoured books about faraway times and places, I learned to wonder what it would take for me to live like the people I was reading about and for my new country to change into yet something else.

A follower of the old political science which, unlike the new, emphasized the variety of human experience, Codevilla was interested in unearthing and examining the different ways men work, engage in civil matters, raise families, worship, and fight. His stated purpose in writing the book became the reintroduction of "the concept of regime to modern readers."

The best minds of antiquity had considered regimes central to understanding human life. And Codevilla had seen for himself the remarkable differences between being raised as a child in post-WWII Italy, then recovering from the ravages of the war, and finally growing into manhood in his new American homeland in the '50s, at that time the most prosperous and admired nation in the world.

At the close of the Cold War a generation later, the American regime was again churning. Yet most American commentators were more concerned with naming and envisaging the contours of the next stage in human history. Should the "post–Cold War" age be defined in terms of a "New World Order," "unipolar moment," "American-led balance of power," or perhaps "the end of history"?

With some important exceptions (most notably Samuel

Huntington's *Clash of Civilizations*), these approaches to understanding the world after the fall of the Soviet Union were misleading as they distracted from serious consideration of the fundamental realities of the human condition. These assessments represented a continuation of many 19th- and 20th-century political and social scientists who offered theories, formulas, and prescriptions that they thought made complete sense of the world or could be rhetorically grafted on it to change it to their preferred order.

Meanwhile, powerful forces were continuing to reshape American politics and culture. That Americans detected in the nineties that life was different was one thing. But if Americans were unaware of why the changes were taking place, they might be blinded to the longer-term consequences of continuing to reshape their regime into something other than what it had been. Codevilla was not spurred on by nostalgia, but rather by his realization that an education in regimes was necessary if Americans were to learn the difference between one regime and another.

With the advantage of having encountered so many ways of life as a young man and political practitioner, Codevilla was hopeful at first to recover the concept of regime by cataloging the varieties of regimes that existed across the world. His editor, Martin Kessler, instead counseled that a better approach would be to flesh out the logic of regimes as explained in the classics of political science, culminating in a focus on the American regime.

Reconfigured thereafter, the dominant theme of the book was to teach Americans that their future would very much be decided by the same forces that shaped every nation's way of life, namely, "the countervailing powers of habit and contingency."

Establishing this theme required beginning with the central teaching of classical political science: that ethics and politics stand as the twin wellsprings of human culture. As the study of ethics teaches the relationship between habits, intellectual and moral virtue, and individual happiness, politics completes this study by placing it within the context of how and what types of regimes produce a more perfect ordering of political communities conducive to happiness, and what types of regimes produce the opposite.

Moreover, Codevilla posited in *The Character of Nations* that history had shown us that fundamental to recovering the concept of regimes was understanding that they operate within civilizational confines:

> Particular regimes bring out some of the potential inherent in any given civilization while suppressing others. Civilizations so limit the influence of regimes that, for example, in civilizations where the God-given equality and worth of individuals is not self-evident, we may not properly use the term "democracy" to describe movements for spreading political power.
>
> ... Within the bounds set by any given civilization, the various broad categories of regimes – tyranny, the several kinds of oligarchy, and democracy – have peculiar effects on the capacity of peoples to be prosperous and civil and to live spiritually meaningful lives in families, free from foreign domination.

That regimes do not form political communities in a vacuum but within the context of a civilization takes on particular importance when examining the evolution of regimes within Western civilization. The first Western political communities were cosmologically unified such that "no distinction had existed among religion, society, and government." In this arrangement, the form and reach of regimes were tied to, in Aristotle's famous formulation, the "arrangement of offices and honors."

As much as Plato and Aristotle emphasized regimes in their presentation of political life, inherent in their philosophic examination of justice is the realization that rulers fall short in meeting "the demands of nature." Likewise, Christ's admonishment that we "render unto Caesar that which is Caesar's, and unto God that which is God's" brings into question loyalty to an earthly regime that has no transcendent and eternal significance. Finally, Rome's collapse led to the development of a new political form, the Holy Roman Empire, and its successor, the Universal Church, in which the sparring between advocates of the competing forces of religion, society, and government took precedence over the regime as the organizing principle of Western political communities. In short, the influence of regimes post-antiquity waned because of the changes produced by philosophic cosmopolitanism, Christianity, and political disintegration.

For Codevilla, these changes played out under the influence of a common prescription that created a healthy constraint upon government. While the regime in its ancient form was not preserved, an equilibrium was established in Christendom through the recognition of a higher law that ordered the relationship between rulers and ruled:

> The Christian commentators combined Jesus' command with Platonic-Aristotelian natural law and gradually produced what might be called the social doctrine of the Christian Middle Ages – a set of ideas and practices that limited the consequences of government.

In modernity, regimes would come to take on a primary role again. The establishment of the political form of the nation-state, empowered by war and its moral equivalents, and endowed with rapidly expanding administrative oversight, made crucial again the question of how "offices and honors" would be arranged within regimes.

How was it then that modern history culminated in the horrors of the 20th century, in which imbalanced regimes led hundreds of millions to their deaths? In exploring this question, Codevilla noted that throughout much of Western Europe and the New World, the democratic polity was the predominant regime eventually established in the modern world. And like other chastened friends of modern democracy, he recognized that democratic regimes could be host to a great variety of arrangements, movements, and political temptations:

> Because democracies have no character except that which their regimes and their peoples combine to give them at any particular time, they can exhibit any of the features of other regimes. And they can change rapidly. The history of the Roman and Athenian democracies, to name but two, is replete with swings between valor and cowardice, poverty and prosperity, freedom and tyranny, piety and sacrilege, harmony and civil war.

According to Codevilla, this reality placed a great responsibility on those living within democratic regimes to play the part of citizens, a part made more challenging in an age defined in large part by the material transformation produced by the unleashed powers of human ingenuity, science, and technology. From this grew one great temptation, encapsulated most memorably by the philosopher Eric Voegelin: the belief that we could create heaven on this earth. Framed within the false constructs of ideologies, many came to believe that cosmological unity was within reach, albeit reduced to its material and mechanistic elements within the modern world.

Here Codevilla argued that a nexus threatens to connect and corrupt men living under modern regimes, from dogmatic modern tyrants and would-be scientific philosopher-kings, to the pleasure-seeking, vitiated multitude operating under their guidance. It promises order and comfort. It asks of men their obeisance. To the degree that the spectatorial mode of life draws men away from acting like citizens, it risks undermining the commitment to equality and liberty that had enabled the establishment of democratic rule in the first place.

In *The Character of Nations*, Codevilla hoped that by closely examining "who rules," "for the good and to the taste of whom," and "to what end," he might apply classical political science to understand the logic of regimes, and then apply this logic to the modern American democratic regime that was perverting our economic, civic, familial, and spiritual lives as well as our commitment to defend our way of life from domestic and foreign enemies.

This pivot would require a return to the fundamental questions that citizens in original regimes asked, namely, "What is the best way of life?" and its writ-large equivalent, "What is justice?" It would also require Americans to recommit to the uniquely American understanding of democratic justice as "an empire of laws, not of men."

> In textbook American discourse, "democracy" means rule by the majority of citizens, all of whom count alike and all of whom have the right to vote and to be elected to office. This understanding of democracy presupposes a willingness on the part of both rulers and ruled to abide by the same laws, to grant unto others the freedoms and powers one expects for oneself, to restrain oneself and one's friends as one would restrain one's opponents. This whole idea makes sense only insofar as one believes that every citizen, regardless of power or status, is both equal and worthy in some fundamental way. With every passing year, however, fewer and fewer within Western civilization believe this.

Though waning, Americans still had the opportunity to consider the differences between regimes, and thereafter choose to live in a citizen-led democratic republic framed by the establishment of laws, customs, and cultural norms. In the example of the American Founding, Americans could draw upon an inheritance greatly influenced by those ancient sensibilities, about the extent and limits of politics given the constraints of human nature, that had helped establish the American regime in the first place.

To revive some semblance of the regime of the American founders in the late 20th century, Americans also would have to root out the new regime, and its corollary way of thinking about politics, that had come to shape elite political opinion. (As Codevilla noted at the end of *The Character of Nations,* "Even in America, there is only one regime at a time.") This effort would require an analysis of what "new modes and orders" were being established in American society, and, in turn, a careful consideration of Niccolò Machiavelli, the thinker who had initiated a hoped-for convergence of philosophy and power in the modern world.

WORDS, POWER, AND MACHIAVELLI'S IMAGINED REPUBLIC AND PRINCIPALITY

While writing *The Character of Nations*, Codevilla was in the process of completing a new translation and edition of Machiavelli's *The Prince,* containing an introduction and four essays placing the Florentine's masterpiece within the context of the Western tradition and the American political experience. Codevilla advanced that Machiavelli's project, pared down to its core, was to subvert the idea of objective truth.

> On the deepest level of all, *The Prince* began the most recent and most revolutionary chapter of the central controversy of our civilization, namely, are our concepts of right and wrong merely reflections of our interests and power or do they reflect, however hazily, the objective order of things, whether natural or divine?

The Prince, Codevilla argued, was the "fountainhead of modern political thought" not because of the events it describes, nor because of the ancient claim it repurposes, but because of the way it was written, a seductive and accessible reconfiguring of morality and politics. While others already had noted this important aspect, it was what Codevilla hoped to make of it that rendered his examination of Machiavelli central to understanding how Machiavelli's influence on the American regime might be mitigated.

In the opening essay of the volume, "Words and Power," Codevilla wrote that it was essential that he, as translator, not "clean up" Machiavelli's prose, whose intention was to purposefully "please a highly partisan, and not too discriminating, Florentine audience." Here Machiavelli departed from the "courtly" language (specifically, the "court of Rome") of Dante because he cared not to use language in a manner that corresponded to reality but to imprint upon his readers a different reality. Language is the most powerful weapon to teach people how not to think reasonably about the most fundamental questions of existence:

> For Dante, the function of language is to describe the nature of things. To the extent that men understand the place of everything in a divinely ordered natural hierarchy, they may attune themselves to reality. Words express men's best understanding of how every piece of reality fits with every other. Therefore, although words are not quite the means of grace, they have much to do with steering men toward saving truth and damning error.

Moreover, language is also the most potent means to get people to act. Freed, unlike Dante, from employing language "to describe the nature of things," Machiavelli set on an artistic course to create a new political and moral universe that encourages people to think of nothing other than actions and how they are viewed by others. Acquisition, administration, maintenance, forceful measures, and soldiery are the definitive features of human life as they correspond to a world that is defined by movement, antagonism, and disorder rather than the pretended constellation of heavenly tranquility and peace.

The most fundamental aspect of Machiavelli's art was to direct his reader's attention away from considering an otherworldly, transcendent moral realm. He sought to accomplish this by dismissing "imagined republics and principalities" as a means by which we might judge human actions. In Chapter XV of *The Prince*, Machiavelli offered a new paradigm to guide our view of the world.

> But, it being my intention to write something useful to him who perceives it, it has appeared to me more convenient to go after the effective truth of the thing rather than the imagination of it. And many have imagined for themselves republics and principalities that no one has ever seen or known in reality. Because how one ought to live is so far removed from how one lives that he who lets go of what is done for that which one ought to do sooner learns his ruin than his own preservation: because a man who might want to make a show of goodness in all things necessarily comes to ruin among so many who are not good.

Codevilla posited that Machiavelli's intention to make a show of badness in all things comes to success by enticingly suggesting to his readers that their actions are not good or bad inherently but effectually. If the sole means of judging human activity is effectual truth, then all measures of right and wrong that are intangible are inconsequential.

Machiavelli's teaching is particularly seductive in that it is accessible to all people, regardless of status. While he highlighted two humors or classes of men found in political communities, the rulers and the ruled, all are accounted for in his anthropology, which reduces human life to its common degradation and need of aggregate utility:

> Because this can be generally said about men: that they are ungrateful, fickle, dissimulators, apt to flee peril, covetous of gain; and while you do them good, they are all

> yours, they offer you their blood, their things, their life, their children, as I said above, when need is far off, but when it draws near to you, they revolt.

While ancient groupings of men (the one, the few, and the many) appear within Machiavelli's rendering of politics, his consistent reduction of all human activity to the self-interested struggle for, or relief from, power attempts to make superfluous a serious discussion of the important differences between types of human beings and regimes.

After describing Machiavelli's impressive use of language, Codevilla asked, much like Socrates did of Thrasymachus in Plato's *Republic*, a simple question:

> The truly compelling feature of the true world, says Machiavelli, the feature that makes it dangerous to live by imagination, is the prevalence of people who are "not good." But by now the inquiring mind has been led to ask, "Not good according to what standard?"

Whereas the problem of what (Machiavellian) men tend to do is not easily resolved, Codevilla offered that it does not close out a discussion of what standards should guide human activity. The difference between how humans *ought* to think, make choices, and live, and how they do has always existed to varying degrees. We must not fall prey to a static understanding of human nature that subsumes the "ought" into the "is" to the point of annihilating the difference between the two.

Codevilla's example teaches that the best way not to be spellbound by Machiavelli's imaginary republic and principality is found in the recovery of ancient political science. We still have it within our means to pursue truth, to reason effectively, and with tangible, real-world examples to show "what men do at any given time depends on what habits they acquired." Human imperfection should not preclude important investigations into how habits, both good and bad, shape the character of men and nations within the exigencies of the human condition.

Codevilla noted that Machiavelli's project has proven largely effective given his extraordinary ability to use words as a means of political conquest. While he, for a time, had been able to "capture" and "conquer" the word virtue, he did not "destroy" virtue.

Although one might allow for the possibility that Machiavelli's attempt to eliminate the transcendent as a human horizon was performed with humane intentions, Codevilla concluded that Machiavelli's ideas have had "lives of their own." In particular, Codevilla argued that Machiavelli could never have imagined that his ideas would have been misemployed by others to make it unfashionable to draw attention to philosophic glory, or be used by his worst adherents to justify their inglorious deeds. Nevertheless, his project must be judged in terms of its terrible consequences, and a response to it formulated in terms of what means might be employed to counter its harmful effects.

MACHIAVELLI'S EXAMPLE

It would be incorrect, however, to conclude that Codevilla rejected Machiavelli's teaching in toto. Codevilla wrote near the end of his introduction that "any reader who habitually plays with this master will be more than ready to deal with run-of-the-mill minds." Political mediocrities could easily be understood through a Machiavellian lens, and we are right to ask what he learned from the "master" that he employed in the service of a better end – and a different master.

While Machiavelli's art consisted in "his ability to change the meaning of words," his primary objective in using words, victory, was unwavering. This prompted him to use language in a manner that would have the broadest appeal, accomplished in part by writing for "a highly partisan and not too discriminating Florentine audience," and in another by embedding ambiguity in his prose. Moreover, he was quick to use words to besmirch and destroy the reputation, and thus status, of others. Machiavelli's contemporaries, bound by custom to employ language politely, were no match for him given his street-smart tactics.

In his own use of language, Codevilla selectively employed some of Machiavelli's methods and repurposed them. He was quick to call out liars, fools, and phonies, highlight their errors, and provide ample evidence of their unsuitability as models of statesmanship. His writing reads more like an exercise in mixed martial arts than a gentlemanly golf match, thus earning him a reputation for being a nasty, brutish, and unphilosophic interlocutor. However, while Machiavelli was interested in "disordering" language and reality, Codevilla's objective was to reorder language by insisting that it correspond to reality. This act required force, intensity, and disdain for ignorance.

Like his teacher Harry Jaffa, Codevilla was willing to anger his audience if his confrontational use of language and blunt analysis drew the well-meaning to uncomfortable yet essential truths about the stakes of human stupidity. Lies, buffoonery, and deception are real, dangerous, and worthy of our reflection, engagement, and contempt. They must be admonished in straightforward terms to the broadest possible audience.

Machiavelli wrote to create a new metaphysics of politics. His task was to reconstitute political reality by blurring distinctions between virtue and vice, good and evil, and right and wrong. Correspondingly, Angelo Codevilla's purpose was to teach politics to an audience that had been misled on a wide variety of the most important aspects of the human experience: war and peace, knowledge and ignorance, truth and falsehood, reality and imagination, and the difference between good and bad thinking, good and bad ideas, good and bad choices, and good and bad consequences. As such, he was compelled to traverse the ground that had been plowed and sown by Machiavelli.

Codevilla sought, unlike Machiavelli, to bring clarity to these most fundamental aspects of human experience. His books on war and foreign policy taught the basics of statecraft, how to operate most successfully within domestic and international environments. This advice, placed within the moral hierarchy of good statesmanship, emphasized making and keeping the regime's peace. For Codevilla, doing well by one regime meant doing what was right by it. These efforts, once again, involved a constant pressure to reorder and simplify the art of statesmanship, which, disordered and obfuscated over time, had been practiced poorly by contemporary so-called experts.

The final and perhaps most interesting of all considerations of Codevillian connection to Machiavelli is discovered in their varying commitment to the common good of their political communities. It is not until Chapter XXVI of *The Prince*, "Exhortation to take Italy and, avenging, free her from the barbarians," that Machiavelli's writing takes on a patriotic bearing. His was a civilizational project that sought to garner him a legacy that extended beyond the reaches of his Florentine republic and Italian nation. Hence there is little or no mention made to bring good to a particular regime until this parting cynical exhortation.

Machiavelli references the armed non-Italian prophets Moses, Cyrus, and Theseus as models for how a new Italian prince might free his country from barbarism. In each instance, the excellence of the statesman corresponds to the level of oppression his people faced. Calling for a new redeemer prince to do the same on the Italian peninsula, Machiavelli closes *The Prince* by quoting Petrarch's famous poem that encouraged Italian unity and peace: "Virtue against furor will take arms; and the fighting be short: for the ancient valor in Italian hearts is not yet dead."

Whereas Machiavelli operates on a philosophic plane throughout *The Prince*, particularizing his cause in terms of Italian political liberation only as a rhetorical means to extend his universal ambitions, Codevilla's writings embody a complete and total commitment to the American regime.

For Codevilla, the masterpieces of philosophy, history, and literature were to be employed in the service of the American regime. Desiring to draw out important axioms from surveying human experience, he praises political excellence displayed across borders and time. Yet Codevilla's ultimate heroes and standard-bearers are Americans. Washington, John Quincy Adams, and Abraham Lincoln show us the way forward because it is in their example that Americans might best learn to blend the usually incompatible elements of public spiritedness and private honor.

Codevilla's emphasis in both *The Character of Nations* and his edition of *The Prince* amounted to an exhortation to Americans to recapture the virtue that propelled the regime to existence. On his account, the true purpose of American nationhood had not been sustained in over a century as American leaders had fallen under universalist spells – echoes of Machiavelli's earlier ambitions – that drew them further away from its republican founding. Only by reconstituting these founding sensibilities and habits, and working within the practical realities of the world as it is, would it be possible to secure a semblance of America's earlier peace.

OUR PRESENT SITUATION

> This is our revolution: Because a majority of Americans now no longer share basic sympathies and trust, because they no longer regard each other as worthy of equal consideration, the public and private practices that once had made our Republic are now beyond reasonable hope of restoration. Strife can only mount until some new equilibrium among us arises.

Despite Codevilla's cautionary warnings two decades earlier, the 21st-century American experience proved to be continually destructive to America's constitutional republic. These years provided Codevilla with an astounding array of historical developments through which to chronicle the country's further decay.

The failed twenty-year "war on terror," the 2008 financial crisis in which elite interests were deemed "too big to fail," the ensuing solidification of "the ruling class," the sullying of "deplorables" who "cling to guns and religion," Donald Trump's sensational yet indecisive effort to "make America great again," "the COVID coup," and "cancel culture." Each further alienated Americans from one another and made them less willing to practice the self-restraint necessary to sustain a healthy republic.

Given that Codevilla's political project had always aimed at restoration and working through regular constitutional channels to defend the American republic, one might ask what he thought was the best course of action once America had moved beyond it.

Some aspects of his counsel would remain the same. If what moved the anti-republican leaders of the new American regime was their disdain for those who still believe the self-evident truth that "All men are created equal" and who recognize "the Laws of Nature and Nature's God," Codevilla advocated rekindling self-assurance among the American people by contesting the claims of those who did not share this faith. This would mean in practice challenging those who fashion idols, and showing confidently how these idols will ultimately be proven unworthy according to the dictates of reason and natural law. Our lives must amount to a demonstrable protest in which we bear witness to the difference between being a self-governing citizen and a subject.

That established, we must face the unfortunate truth that our constitutional republic is beyond repair. This requires clarity as to the nature of the progressive oligarchic regime, and the likelihood that it will allow Americans of a different persuasion to pursue a way of life that conflicts with its commitments. In "Revolution 2020," Angelo wrote:

> The longer we pretend to live under precisely the same laws, the likelier we will end up killing one another. We must not do that. And yet regional differences notwithstanding, we are mostly intermingled. Sorting ourselves

> into compatible groups is part of the American genius and tradition. More of that has been happening and more will happen yet. If we want to live in peace, as we should, we must contrive to agree to disagree to accommodate peace.

Whether the resorting of the American political landscape will allow for this détente is another matter. Will ruling-class progressives carry out the demands of *intersectionals* who desire the absolute de-Americanization of all *deplorables* or, lacking the requisite will, instead practice a resigned neglect in which they make allowances for Americans to "agree to disagree"?

Codevilla's recommendation, if possible, was to do no harm. The aim of a non-Machiavellian American statesman must be a peace in which adherents to the founders' regime are given the opportunity to live as Americans. Although hopeful for an outcome in which would-be combatants choose not to go to war, his advice in "On the Natural Law of War and Peace" was clear: "If you have to fight to preserve or reestablish your peace, then fight with all you've got to accomplish that as quickly as possible."

We fervently desire that a new American political equilibrium not be established by bloodshed. To Codevilla's main teaching, the surest way to secure the American regime for our posterity is to live out its commitments to liberty and justice for all. Though a political haze may cover the United States for a time, Americans must continue to keep watch with the recognition that as the truth, goodness, and justice they look for is real, they labor not in vain.

STEVEN F. HAYWARD

THE COMPLEAT POLITICAL THINKER

ANGELO CODEVILLA ON "WHAT ARE WE DOING TO OURSELVES?"

> *Today in America, as throughout the West, government has become arguably the major source of society's decay.*
>
> ANGELO CODEVILLA,
> *America's Rise and Fall Among Nations*

IN AN IMAGINARY WORLD in which foreign conflict and military strategy didn't exist, Angelo Codevilla, best known for his work on grand strategy, intelligence, and arms control, would instead have emerged as one of the premier social thinkers of our era, mentioned in the same breath alongside James Q. Wilson or Edward Banfield. He had much the same originality and candor. And when observed from Codevilla's perspective on domestic political affairs, a familiar intellectual dichotomy of modern, so-called scientific politics – the division of foreign policy from domestic policy – is entirely wrongheaded, and is yet another means of diminishing the proper role of political argument in public affairs.

The old cliché of partisan differences ending at the water's edge was never true, but the illusion of it buttressed the pretensions and claims to rule of an expert class whose dominant traits are a narrowness of view and ideological conformity. And though often papered over, partisan divisions of the Cold War era were just as, if not more, bitter than today's domestic political disputes. It may seem a larger amount of bipartisan continuity can be ascribed to Cold War foreign policy ("containment," for example) while domestic politics featured more rancor and policy instability between parties, but in fact both spheres were deeply polarized, and the philosophical and epistemological sources of the divisions are identical once we look beneath the surface.

At the same time, most leading foreign-policy specialists of the Cold War era – or really any era – are out of their depth on domestic policy. Just try to conjure up Henry Kissinger or Hans Morgenthau having something serious to say about welfare, crime, housing, family, or tax-rate policies. Not even George Kennan in his semi-conservative moralist mode had much intelligent to say about domestic politics. Codevilla had lots to say about these matters.

Codevilla thus provides us with a rare example of the unity of statecraft, of the reciprocal relation between domestic and foreign politics, most comprehensively in his 1997 book *The Character of Nations: How Politics Makes and Breaks Prosperity, Family, and Civility*. Though more than twenty-five years old, *The Character of Nations* holds up for the same reasons Tocqueville holds up, both for its depth on the fundamentals as well as its prescience: "the character of the American way of life is up for grabs perhaps more than ever before," such that "a generation from now we might well live in yet another kind of country." That "another kind of country" has arrived. It might well be said that just as Codevilla fought against MAD (mutual assured destruction) in arms control and strategic nuclear doctrine, he also fought against the madness gripping our political and cultural elites in domestic matters.

Little more than a decade after *The Character of Nations*, Codevilla outlined just how America was hardening into "another kind of country" with his essay – later a book – on "The Ruling Class." His critique went well beyond the usual pointing to unaccountable bureaucratic government ruling in its own interest against the majority opinion of Americans. He "went there," as the saying goes: "The Republican Party did not disparage the ruling class, because most of its officials are or would like to be part of it." Anticipating Donald Trump (about whom he had mixed views), Codevilla charged that Republicans were too willing to be junior partners to Democrats in the ruling class.

And in a sense, Codevilla updated *The Character of Nations* with his final book, posthumously published in 2022, *America's Rise and Fall Among Nations: Lessons in Statecraft from John Quincy Adams*. Although this was chiefly a work explaining the increasing weakness of American strategy and status in the world, he could not help but notice the essential connection between the causes of American civil society's enfeeblement. The central chapter of this otherwise outward-facing book peers inward to highlight the significance of an intelligentsia who regard so many of their fellow citizens as "deplorables."

One of Codevilla's greatest talents was cutting through the prevailing sentimental nonsense and clichés that attempt to confine and pre-determine policy and strategy. About détente – the bipartisan doctrine of the 1970s – Codevilla saw that it was essentially Appeasement 2.0, writing: "Détente was a sophisticated attempt to bribe the Soviets not to use their guns." Likewise, his conclusion on why the Soviet Union collapsed in 1991 eschewed all of the sophisticated intellectual constructs about "modernization," "convergence," or mere economic sclerosis: "The proximate cause of the collapse was the Communists' waning will to murder."

In accordance with Codevilla's statecraft, we should never think a problem can be solved by converting fundamental issues into technical ones, which was his central critique of the arms control "process" with the Soviet Union, but also the premise behind the scientific politics of the administrative state since the Progressive Era a century ago. In other words, we make the same category error as arms control with domestic politics, thinking new infusions of money, a new state or federal program, or a new administrative entity is the primary remedy for any social problem. Additional funds are sometimes useful, such as hiring more police and building prisons to get habitual criminals off the street, but much of the time these grand new initiatives merely expand bureaucracies for intractable social problems and provide still more organizational platforms for claims of authority.

The "arms control community," and its self-asserted claim to moral and foreign policy authority, finds its close domestic analogue in the "welfare rights" and related social policy advocacy groups (especially "homeless services," whose existence and "success" depends on the number of homeless increasing). This style of political activity aims at more than just commanding more financial resources. It aims above all to control our discourse about the issues, knowing that controlling the definition of key terms and accepted language will help determine the direction of policy. A good example of this linguistic shift can be seen in how the older term "juvenile delinquent" or "juvenile offender" has now become, in officialese, "justice-involved youth," which has bolstered in turn the move to lax criminal enforcement and sentencing, and a predictable rise in crime committed by youth.

We may understand Codevilla's disposition to plain and direct pronouncements as translated to domestic politics starting with the premise of *The Character of Nations*, which is straightforward: there is a logic to modern regimes, and this logic affects America as much as any other regime. Codevilla seldom if ever used the term "American exceptionalism" in his work, and if he ever mentioned it in a speech, it would be first to snort about the superficiality of the phrase as it has come to be used and overused. It is not that he thought America and the founding were not exceptional. Rather, he understood that too many people who champion "American exceptionalism" for the right reasons nonetheless commit an error to suppose the unique character of America's founding makes us immune to the forces that can ruin a nation and a people.

Following the example of Machiavelli, his writing has a way of seeing familiar problems in a new context and with different vocabulary. It mustn't be overlooked that Codevilla produced his own excellent translation of *The Prince*, published in 1997, the same year as *The Character of Nations*, which rivals Harvey Mansfield's better-known translation for its literalness and explication of linguistic subtleties for readers not familiar with Italian. The two translations track each other closely, but differ on some fine points of rendering Italian terms into English in ways that express what each translator thinks is more faithful to Machiavelli's shadings.

For example, there are several subtle differences in how Mansfield and Codevilla translate key terms in the famous 15th chapter, on "imaginary republics" and the "effectual truth" of politics, starting with the title of the chapter itself. Mansfield: "Of Those Things for Which Men and Especially Princes Are Praised or *Blamed*." Codevilla: "Of those things for which men, and especially princes, are lauded or *vilified*." (Emphasis added throughout.) Mansfield renders the Italian "modi e governi" in the opening sentence as "modes and *government*," while Codevilla renders it "modes and *rules*." "Government" is more literal, but "rules" draws us to what government does rather than invoking a general institutional shape. The ways each translates the third sentence of the chapter show how carefully the two regard the profundity and grace of Machiavelli's writing, which is crucial to interpreting his thought and intention. Mansfield: "But since my intent is to write something useful to whoever *understands* it, it has appeared to me more *fitting* to go directly to the effectual truth of the thing than to the imagination of it." Codevilla: "But, it being my intention to write something useful to him who *perceives* it, it has appeared to me more *convenient* to go after the effective truth of the thing rather than the imagination of it." (Again, emphasis added.) Codevilla adds this useful explanatory footnote: "Machiavelli does not say 'a chi se ne intende,' i.e., 'to him who knows what he is doing.' Nor does he say he wants to 'dare da intendere,' i.e., to put something over on the reader. Rather, he will speak straight to whomever is able to follow him." Codevilla and Mansfield are not simply working carefully with the text; both share an awareness, controversial among conventional scholars, that Machiavelli fully perceived the ironic and esoteric teaching of Plato but aimed to redirect political thought not only more realistically but explicitly.

In the introduction to his translation, Codevilla reminds us of the core Machiavellian teaching that "language is fundamentally a weapon in human struggles," because language "consists of changing the terms in which people think." As if in anticipation of today's speech codes and the attempts to control terms of discourse, Codevilla wrote: "If a language is so structured as to make impossible the articulation of certain thoughts, those thoughts, Machiavelli contends, will be banished forever from the minds of those who speak that language." Behold our current condition in which the basic term "woman" has become contested, and even the term "immigrants" – instead of illegal aliens – is judged too pejorative by progressive sensibilities, and thus they are now called "newcomers." The corruption of language is the surface manifestation of how the broader idea that one can create one's own "values" or identity *ex nihilo* has gone from heresy to official orthodoxy, complete with strong social sanctions – and perhaps legal sanctions in the fullness of time – for using an incorrect pronoun.

Codevilla's understanding of this problem differs in important respects from many other theoretical and practical conservative attempts to explain it, such as by the pretense of expertise and the constitutional degradation of the separation of powers inherent in the administrative state. And although Codevilla professes to prefer the classical political science of Aristotle to modern political science and to write "political science in the old style," he notes that it is necessary to understand modern politics through a Machiavellian lens or, to adopt the popular title by another author, that we live in a Machiavellian moment in which the rulers seek to introduce new modes and orders.

We can best appreciate how his perspective and discussion differs by noting how, at a late moment in *The Character of Nations*, Codevilla brings up the most salient fact about long-term trends in American public opinion – "the trust question." Starting in the late 1950s, Gallup, Harris, and other major polling organizations began asking some version of "Do you have confidence or trust in the federal government?" When this question was introduced, the number of Americans who expressed confidence or trust in the federal government to do the right thing was around 80 percent. Today, the number languishes around 15 percent.

It has been all downhill since the mid-1960s, with only one period of sustained reversal – the Reagan years – but even then not back to the heights of civic confidence seen in the 1950s. The standard explanation for this is the growth of government alongside its obviously declining competence. And there is much to this explanation with which Codevilla would agree. It is not a coincidence that public confidence in the federal government began its precipitous decline in the mid-1960s, when the government embarked on two large-scale wars that it lost – in Vietnam overseas and on poverty at home, both conceived largely as social-engineering projects. In fact, some of the same people from the go-go days of confident liberalism worked on designing the policy for both wars.

But to Codevilla these and subsequent failures are not the consequence primarily of constitutional decay, regulatory hubris, fiscal recklessness, or even centralization. Culpable is the deeply corrupted culture of the administrative state, whose tendrils have reached even the lowest level of local government today, which may actually be worse than in Washington, DC, as in the case of the Coralville, Iowa, police who shut down four-year-old Abigail Krutsinger's sidewalk lemonade stand in 2013 because she lacked a $400 city permit. Such a feat was then duplicated in Midway, Georgia; Appleton, Wisconsin; McAllen, Texas; and more than three dozen other cities across the country that were reported in the media. Some parents were slapped with

$500 fines for allowing their kids to sell lemonade without the proper permits. Local bureaucracies have even restricted or stopped annual Girl Scout cookie sales drives.

The COVID-lockdown lunacy exposed this authoritarian impulse in grotesque fashion. Local governments didn't just close parks and other public spaces but even rendered them unusable by acts that would otherwise be understood as vandalism, such as pouring sand in skate parks and nailing boards across basketball rims in playgrounds. The ultimate absurdity was the Los Angeles County sheriff's deputies arresting a lone surfer in Malibu. This kind of idiocy did not require pressure from the national government. Local governments were only too eager to embrace their own self-generated idiocy.

There is an almost malevolent character of our government's incompetence. A government that cannot, for example, keep dangerous, insane people off subways can nonetheless undertake to control the temperature of the planet by expending a few trillion dollars, banning your gas stove, and requiring everyone to drive an electric car in the near future. The latest answer to urban traffic congestion is bike lanes that almost no one uses, but which remove entire lanes of traffic and scarce streetside parking on already-packed roads. Was there enormous popular demand for bike lanes? Did local government candidates run on bike lanes as a leading issue? Of course not: they are the fever dream of elite planners, imposed through the usual drip of interminable regulatory and "planning" processes kept deliberately opaque to the public.

Another remarkable example: California is considering legislation that would outlaw tobacco over the next two decades, while leaving marijuana untouched. At the same time, government regulation and taxes have made the legal marijuana trade unprofitable – something the government was unable to do with alcohol when Prohibition ended. It's as though our rulers really don't like how we live and are determined to change our bad habits.

Worth special attention because it seems, on the surface, to run against type at present, while sensible people recoil against the "defund the police" nonsense that emerged from the Black Lives Matter hysteria, Angelo was early in perceiving how policing in America had fallen prey to the same bureaucratizing tendencies and oppositional culture that afflicts the EPA or other hotbeds of authoritarian government power. Policing and especially criminal prosecution has been enveloped by the ethos of the ruling class. "Unionization helped to insulate [police] from complaints," Codevilla wrote, "and bureaucratization and the expansion of their jurisdictions insulated them from their fellow citizens."

Policing was once a working-class occupation, with "Officer Murphy" walking the neighborhood beat and sometimes preserving public order by enforcing the unwritten law of the street with means that today would result in misconduct charges (swatting a miscreant with a billy club, for example). But policing became highly professionalized, and in turn highly bureaucratized. Police today talk less like citizens and more like bureaucrats, with the same specialized language that old-time Officer Murphy would never have used.

Supreme Court rulings of the Warren Court era, such as *Miranda* and *Mapp v. Ohio*, contributed significantly to the bureaucratization of policing, but it would likely have happened for the same reason we have experienced bike-lane tyranny. Codevilla explained, "American police in general seem to have designated as their main enemy – as the criminal they cannot tolerate – the citizens who protect themselves. In fact, the police have effectively lobbied for the disarmament of law-abiding citizens and for punishment of those who 'take the law into their own hands.'" Thus, in our increasingly unsafe cities, "courts have consistently held individuals acting in undeniable self-defense liable for injuries to the assailant."

Behold the current spectacle of New York's subways, where, in the absence of any attempt to keep order, a citizen (the US Marines veteran Daniel Penny) who defended himself and his fellow citizens underwent criminal prosecution because an attempt to restrain a violent criminal with a chokehold resulted in the unfortunate death of that deranged individual – who had repeatedly been released from custody by New York City's "justice" system.

On occasion, however, the public wholly rejects this malevolent mindlessness, as in the recent instance of the bodega owner in Manhattan who stabbed a violent assailant in self-defense. After a massive outcry, the district attorney dismissed charges against the owner. Our attention should likewise now be fixed on the astounding spectacle of Great Britain's government and police forces, who doggedly target the native British citizens daring to protest, or even complain on social media, about the mayhem that hordes of culturally hostile immigrants have brought to the sceptered isle.

To those who think this Orwellian nightmare cannot happen here, note the disproportion between the lax or non-existent prosecution of Black Lives Matter rioters from the summer of 2020 and the harsh penalties the Justice Department sought against non-violent protestors who entered the grounds of the US Capitol building on January 6, 2021. This, coming from the same set of elites who refused to accept the results of the 2016 election and went to extraordinary lengths to negate the result of the election by the contrived Russia hoax and the subsequent lawfare campaign against President Donald Trump.

This asymmetry can be explained by a simple fact: billions in property damage is seen as inconsequential, while citizens protesting a dubious election result are a potential threat to the ruling class that must be deterred in the future through draconian enforcement. "Never before has it been so important for Americans to be on the right side of the right people," Codevilla wrote in *America's Rise and Fall*, "and so costly to cross them."

The lack of public trust is not simply a matter of governmental competence. The corollaries of this problem – "polarization" we call it, along with indicators of increasing public rudeness and general abrasiveness such as road rage, "Karenism" (asking for the manager), and the like – are discussed with a clinical sterility that avoids the heart of the matter.

We could forgive incompetence, mistakes, and failures by the government if it weren't so easy to discern that the dominant ethos of our ruling class is a wholesale hostility to the American middle class. Sure enough, Codevilla writes about the trust gap in *The Character of Nations*: "The gap would not have grown so large had there not been a growing recognition by rulers and ruled of the differences in manners and morals – and a growing mutual dislike." In his updated summary of the problem in *America's Rise and Fall*, he puts the matter even more starkly: "The administration that came into office in 2021 officially accuses its opponents of deep-rooted racism, and states that rooting out widespread White Supremacy is its foremost preoccupation … . Americans now view their rulers as corrupt, even when they are not, and as enemies, even when they are not."

Codevilla explains at length how our government is hostile to the family. But this is itself rooted in a larger hostility to religion and the heritage of Western civilization. Codevilla is aligned with Roger Scruton's summary description of our "culture of repudiation" – he does not wonder that our public nastiness has increased proportionally with our growing spiritual emptiness, the consequence of two generations of growing government hostility to America's religious heritage:

> Near worship of abortion and disdain for religion (theophobia) are the principal totems of the vast and wealthy subculture associated with government – most office holders of both parties and the bureaucracies – the leadership of most corporations, the education establishment, the media, etc. These define themselves largely by looking down on the rest of America. Asserting very specific preferences with regard to just about everything – codes of behavior, of language required or banned – they make it a

> point to impress a sense of inferiority on those they consider to be of lower classes.

One of his examples was President Barack Obama's demanding that the crucifix on the wall of the Georgetown University lecture hall where he chose to give a speech be covered up. If Angelo were here to update *The Character of Nations* today, he would certainly point to the wanton destruction of public monuments, understanding that what ostensibly began as a move limited to monuments erected to Confederate figures from the Civil War would not be confined to those problematic memorials, with subsequent "protests" targeting public monuments indiscriminately, including even those honoring Frederick Douglass. Speaking of the Civil War, you can count Codevilla among those who think the United States is indeed in "a cold but warming civil war" fanned by "government-led or -approved attacks on dissenters rais[ing] the prospect of a civil war less like nineteenth-century America's and more like the twentieth-century Spanish horror."

This kind of bracing but plausible speculation (Codevilla notes how much private gun ownership has soared over the last decade) should make it clear that his work is implicitly contemptuous of much of what constitutes the "mainstream" conservative movement of the last two generations, at least on the top priorities of public policy. A lot of the ideas conservatives promote most prominently today are small beer and largely irrelevant to the cultural crisis – you might ironically call it a Bud Lite strategy. Overturn the Chevron doctrine; install real cost–benefit analysis for regulation; require congressional approval for major regulations through the REINS Act; a balanced budget and tax cuts *uber alles* – all good and sensible policy ideas, all worthy of support. None comes close to a remedy for the cultural and intellectual rot gripping the nation.

Conservatives need something bold that will provoke debate about fundamentals. Codevilla's disposition on the domestic scene inspires three ideas.

First, we need a truly robust pro-family policy. Codevilla notes that Japan has tax policies that favor single-earner households (and those beloved social Democracies of Scandinavia have tax policies that are more pro-family than America's). The best our team can do right now is propose an expanded child tax credit, now embraced by J. D. Vance. How about going big with a policy that says, for example, that intact two-parent families with three or more children shall be completely exempt from the income tax, and maybe the payroll tax as well. Imagine the howls of the cultural Left over that. (I'll add that Codevilla hints that maybe we ought to consider bringing back the traditional practice of "shotgun weddings.") A similar pro-family tax policy in Hungary appears to have increased the birth rate over the past decade since it was adopted.

Second, one of Codevilla's worries, derived from his unified field of view, is that a government that cannot perform its most basic tasks such as ensuring the safety of our cities, the competence of our public schools, or the maintenance of basic infrastructure will likewise prove unable to defend the country from a serious foreign threat. He is not the first to point out that military service as a proportion of the citizenry is at a century-long low point.

Serious consideration of the idea of national service (or even the military draft, with no exemptions for Harvard students) needs to be made. And I don't mean goo-goo national service like AmeriCorps where you work in a recycling center on a college campus, but a national service that emphasizes military training, like the Swiss and Israelis have. It is not a coincidence that Codevilla echoes Machiavelli in saying the Swiss are "the most armed and the most free." He discusses the Swiss experience at some length in *The Character of Nations*; the Swiss do not have a martial reputation, but perhaps their universal service and training requirement (and gun-ownership requirement) are among the reasons for this paradox. There are huge practical difficulties with this idea in the more pluralistic United States, but the howls of fascism from the Left that would greet such a proposal is one reason to recommend it.

Finally, given that the core of the cultural Left is a hatred of religion, perhaps we might think more aggressively of attempting a direct counterattack. And there might be some potential help from a sympathetic Supreme Court. In recent years the Court has, in its usual halting and confused way, been friendly to religious liberty and pushed back against government discrimination against religion, though these are always narrow rulings. It might be possible to conceive of a congressional statute in some policy domain – adoption might be the best realm, but don't overlook school choice or social-service provision – that would compel the Supreme Court to confront and repudiate the secular hostility to religion and religious institutions.

Ronald Reagan used to talk of bringing back school prayer, but never pushed any concrete measures to bring this about. Here's one: Harry Jaffa once noted that forty-nine of the fifty state constitutions mention God or the deity as the source of our rights in their preambles, echoing the language of the Declaration of Independence. A state or federal statute requiring public school children to recite the preambles to their state constitutions every morning would ignite the Left's outrage, but could they with a straight face argue that their own constitutions are unconstitutional? Blue states might move to amend their state charters removing these preambles. Let them instigate this debate, and expose their hostility to religion more directly.

Beyond these and other specific radical ideas lies the heart of the matter, the essential unifying issue for Codevilla: the necessity of high statesmanship. Codevilla's understanding of the difficulties of politics and high statesmanship didn't rest on theoretical study. He was a keen observer of Charles de Gaulle, whose political story combined elements of glory and immiseration. De Gaulle once said of America's Progressives, "They are not serious people." Codevilla adds his own gloss: "Seriousness – what parents look for in a son-in-law – is statesmanship's minimal requirement. Contemporary American statesmen don't rise to the minimum."

Codevilla even hints that he thinks de Gaulle a greater statesman than Churchill, a heresy in the conservative Anglosphere, but in the end even de Gaulle dissipated his reputational capital because he forgot the central truth that politics is about ideas and the soul. A politics that neglects ideas and the soul is doomed to fail: "When one speaks for one's country, it seems, one must speak in terms which can make rightful claims upon men's faith ... Surely no question ever haunted de Gaulle through the years more than that of whether the French people still had it in them to *be* a nation."

That is the central question facing America today.

DAVID P. GOLDMAN

ANGELO CODEVILLA'S FAILURE, AND OURS

In September 2004, just as the George W. Bush administration bet the farm on exporting democracy to the Middle East, NBC News reported: "'I think the neoconservative moment has passed,' says Angelo Codevilla, a conservative foreign policy analyst who helped choose Ronald Reagan's first Cabinet. 'The ideology has worn out its welcome because it has proven impossible to implement. Its foot soldiers will pay the price.'" That was perhaps the worst prediction from one of the most prescient American analysts of the second half of the 20th century. There followed, of course, the forced adoption of majority rule in Iraq, the toppling of America's ally Hosni Mubarak in Egypt, the overthrow and killing of Muammar Qaddafi, the CIA's support for jihadists seeking to overthrow the Assad regime in Syria, and the inevitable results: the rise of extraterritorial Iranian power and the emergence of ISIS as a non-state actor in place of the Sunni state in Iraq that we had destroyed. Popular outrage against "forever wars" was a key factor in Donald Trump's improbable rise to power, but during his first term the foreign-policy establishment remained in charge of his national-security apparatus: H. R. McMaster and John Bolton at the National Security Council, and Gina Haspel at the Central Intelligence Agency.

At this writing, America is bogged down in yet another neoconservative war in Ukraine, with the universal support of the establishment media from the *New York Times* to the *Wall Street*

Journal. The few dissenting voices – for example, Tucker Carlson – are relegated to alternate or social media. The Ukraine morass absorbs American treasure but not blood, and thus elicits less outrage from a population that is taxed but not deployed to fight. Nonetheless, it is remarkable that two decades after the United States set out to gift democracy to the world whether it wanted democracy or not, the same policy and the same people prevail.

The elite remain in power by default. Angelo Codevilla was their most persistent and energetic critic. He was an aristocrat of the mind, with extraordinary breadth of knowledge and deep insight in disparate fields of study. What he could not do was reproduce himself.

A dichotomy ran through Codevilla's career. He played a central and indispensable role in America's turn towards a war-winning strategy under Ronald Reagan, as one of a half-dozen visionaries who early on embraced and championed what became the Strategic Defense Initiative (SDI). In this regard, he exemplified what a well-informed, philosophically grounded, and historically perceptive elite can accomplish. He and his co-thinkers, though, were pushed out of positions of power during the second Reagan administration.

Codevilla's 2010 manifesto, *The Ruling Class: How They Corrupted America and What We Can Do About It*, excoriated the bipartisan elite and projected a revolt by a "country party," whose emergence he hailed in 2014:

> The Republican Party died during the struggle over Obamacare. Its most vital elected officials chose to represent their voters. This left their erstwhile leaders to continue pursuing acceptance by the ruling party, its press and its class. The result is a new party that represents roughly three-fourths of Republican voters whose social identities are alien to those of the ruling class and whose political identity is defined by opposition to the ruling party. These voters are outsiders to modern America's power structure.

> Hence the new party that represents them is a "country party" in the British tradition of Viscount Bolingbroke's early eighteenth century Whigs, who represented the country class against the royal court and its allies in Parliament. The forthcoming food fight over the name "Republican" is of secondary importance.

If Donald Trump did not exist, Codevilla would have had to invent him. No more prescient reading of American politics can be found in the years preceding Trump's election.

Yet Codevilla himself was an elitist of a different kind. He was not only a political philosopher of great depth (among other things, a student of Leo Strauss and Harry Jaffa at the Claremont Graduate School) and a learned translator of Machiavelli, but also by training a physicist. That combination gave him the competence and self-confidence to embrace strategic missile defense in the late 1970s and to play a decisive role in its adoption by the Reagan administration. As governor of California, Ronald Reagan first met Edward Teller, the father of America's hydrogen bomb, in 1967. The great physicist "shared with Reagan his research on using explosives to defend against a nuclear attack. In Reagan's first year in public office, these two historic men met on what would become a historic idea," reports Paul Kengor in *The Crusader: Ronald Reagan and the Fall of Communism*.

Remarkably, Teller's correspondence with Codevilla began in 1962, according to the University of California's catalogue of Teller's papers. If the catalogue is correct, Codevilla, then a nineteen-year-old undergraduate physics student at Rutgers, wrote to and received a response from one of the field's greatest living practitioners. With his former high-school classmates Eugene Wigner and John von Neumann, Teller had pioneered the atomic bomb. The correspondence continued through 1985.

Codevilla served as a naval officer, earned a PhD from the Claremont Graduate School, and in 1977 joined the Foreign Service, but he soon left for Capitol Hill. Rebecca Slayton reports:

"In late 1977, Maxwell Hunter, an aeronautical engineer at Lockheed with a longstanding interest in space vehicles, wrote a paper titled 'Strategic Dynamics and Space-Laser Weaponry.' After circulating it internally at Lockheed, he passed it on to Angelo Codevilla, a member of Wyoming senator Malcolm Wallop's staff." With the help of Hunter and Codevilla, Wallop published an article titled "Opportunities and Imperatives of Ballistic Missile Defense" in *Strategic Review*, claiming that "several dozen laser weapons systems deployed in space would revolutionize the strategic equation as we have known it for nearly two decades – above all by decisively tipping the balance of modern warfare in favor of the defense and radically mitigating the potential destructive effects of war."

It is hard to exaggerate the boldness of Codevilla's initiative, or the importance of his championing missile defense at a crucial juncture. Reagan's friendship with Teller predisposed him to the concept, but the majority of his advisors thought it impractical. In 1983 – after Reagan had announced SDI in a March televised address – his science advisor George Keyworth convened a meeting of physicists at Miami's Fontainebleau Hotel. Keyworth began a session by stating that although the president had publicly declared his support for missile defense, it should be understood that the applications of directed-energy weapons to warfare were unlikely to have practical importance in the foreseeable future. Teller, who walked with a cane after a youthful accident, rose to his full height, swung his cane, and brought it down with full force on the top of his desk. "I will not participate in a meeting that promotes treason!" the great physicist shouted. The startled participants gathered their papers and left the room.

Within and around the administration, a tiny circle of Reagan loyalists backed SDI against majority opposition. These included Codevilla, then a senior staffer of the Senate Select Committee on Intelligence; the national security advisor William Clark, who had served under Governor Reagan; Clark's successor Robert McFarlane; Herbert Meyer, the leader of "Team B" at the CIA, which refuted conventional wisdom about the strength of the Soviet economy; and Norman A. Bailey, a senior NSC staffer for whom I consulted at the time. None of them occupied positions of prominence after the first Reagan administration. Already in decline and back-footed by the Iran–Contra scandal, Reagan turned his second term over to the establishment.

One marvels at the boldness, even arrogance of the thirty-four-year-old Codevilla of 1977, importuning the federal government for a massive commitment of resources to a theoretically plausible but untested scientific hypothesis. As a practical matter, Codevilla required the full resources of the state. But philosophically, he viewed the scientific state with deep hostility. In his 2020 essay on Mussolini, "The Original Fascist," Codevilla wrote:

> European elites had been worshiping the state's architectonic powers since the time of Louis XIV's ministers (Louvois, Vauban, Colbert). G. W. F. Hegel, following Napoleon, had made patriotic worship of the scientifically administered, progressive state the political essence of modernity. Mussolini's vision of Italy followed from that. "The bureaucracy is the state," he said.

But no exercise in American history exemplified the scientifically administered state more than the Manhattan Project, which launched Big Science as a factor in policymaking, embedded in dozens of federal agencies and national laboratories, protected from outside scrutiny by security classification, self-regulating, self-perpetuating, and convinced of its right to govern without kibitzing by *hoi polloi*. Teller, the director of Lawrence Livermore Laboratory, personified Big Science. Although Ernest Lawrence, the founding father of Big Science, was a South Dakotan, it drew on the great migration of European scientists like Teller, Eugene Wigner, John von Neumann, Theodore von Kármán, Hans Bethe, and later Wernher von Braun.

America had imported a generation's worth of the scientific

core of the Hegelian administrative state. The Manhattan Project was its first great success; the Strategic Defense Initiative was its final, abortive sally. By the time that the young Codevilla embraced Edward Teller's concept of strategic defense, most of Teller's wartime colleagues were gone. Kármán died in 1963, von Neumann in 1957, Leo Szilard in 1964. Wigner lived on until 1995 but was inactive after the mid-1960s.

Codevilla was offered, and declined, a seat at the big table. In 2019 he told the journalist David Samuels:

> When I started working for the Senate, some folks at the [Central Intelligence] Agency figured out that I wasn't a run-of-the-mill staffer. So I was visited by one of the old boys who took me up to the director's office – the director wasn't there at the time. He took me up via the director's elevator, he had a key. And showed me all around and was very, very clubby with me. Then they took me to his house, which is overlooking the Potomac, with these large wolfhounds sitting about. And essentially, he said the equivalent of "all this could be yours" … if you play the game. I said to myself, "Hmmmm, what did the Lord say to all this?"
>
> But it really is a matter of who has dinner with whom. I have worked in Washington long enough to know that people would sell their souls for invitations to be at certain tables. To be allowed to speak with this person or that. In the end, it's all social.
>
> And how do you become social? You express the same thoughts, you have the same tastes. You vacation in the same places. You love the same loves, you hate the same hates.

Codevilla's above account is incomplete. Reagan's CIA director was William J. Casey, whose views were close to Codevilla's. The late Herbert Meyer, the vice-chairman of the CIA's National

Intelligence Council under Casey, told me that the CIA made more than one attempt to onboard Codevilla but was rebuffed. Evidently, Codevilla could not bear to become part of the scientific–military–intelligence establishment, even under leaders who generally shared his views. He chose to remain on Capitol Hill and on the periphery of policymaking.

The battle that played out for America's strategic direction after the Vietnam disaster was fought among insiders. Vietnam discredited the concept of strategic equilibrium maintained by limited wars that Henry Kissinger championed. The success of Russian surface-to-air missiles in Vietnam and during the 1973 Arab–Israeli War challenged America's lead in military technology. The revolution in defense technology that ultimately won the Cold War began in 1977 under Jimmy Carter's defense secretary, Harold Brown, the former president of Caltech and one of the country's most distinguished physicists. Although Brown echoed Kissinger in matters of arms control, he also presided over a wave of innovation that carried over into the Reagan administration and inaugurated the Digital Age. We might not have won the Cold War without him.

Codevilla's contempt for the foreign-policy establishment was crystallized in his critique of Henry Kissinger, whose zero-sum-game view of geopolitics excluded the possibility of an American victory in the Cold War. After Admiral Zumwalt's 1976 memoirs attributed a defeatist view to Kissinger, Ronald Reagan had made Kissinger's brand of détente an issue in his unsuccessful challenge to Gerald Ford in that year's presidential primary.

In a 2015 review-essay, "The World According to Kissinger," Codevilla wrote:

> [Kissinger's book] *World Order*, then, inadvertently explicates the source of our ruling class's disorder: a clerisy has escaped the duties and limits inherent in the role of one nation's public servants, entrusted to advance its citizens' security and happiness, in order to carry out imagined

global obligations with assumed capabilities. This failure to discharge true duties for the sake of false ones is why America lost the Vietnam War; discarded its defenses against air and missile attack; sought to keep together a Soviet Union that was coming apart; wasted its superior forces in conflicts without end; cowers as terrorists surround it; and backpedals in the Pacific. Nowadays, we speak of America's renunciation of power as if it were a recent phenomenon. But, grosso modo, it has been the story of US foreign policy for over half a century, and was a glimmer in the eyes of ruling-class intellectuals long before then...

The closest he comes to accounting for world disorder is to note that a system can, like Vienna's, lose "legitimacy." The concept of "legitimacy" – the belief that existing arrangements are not just tolerable but worth defending for their own sake – turns out to be a puffed-up, tautological way of saying that certain arrangements secure favor because people favor them...

[Woodrow] Wilson's career "would appear more the stuff of Shakespearean tragedy than of foreign policy textbooks." And yet he writes that Wilson "had touched an essential chord in the American soul." "[H]e rallied the tradition of American exceptionalism behind a vision that outlasted [his]...shortcomings." Whenever America has faced challenges, "it has returned in one way or another to Woodrow Wilson's vision of a world order that secures peace through democracy, open diplomacy, and the cultivation of shared rules and standards." Nevertheless, Kissinger notes that this "elevated foreign policy doctrine" is "unmoored from a sense of history or geopolitics." Later, when discussing John F. Kennedy, *Kissinger also observes that Wilsonian foreign policy – essentially the foreign policy of the past hundred years – "based the moral universalism of the leaders on the American people's dedication to freedom*

> *and democracy." Note: the people want one thing, which the leaders reinterpret and use to pursue the different thing they want. This is a massive critique* [emphasis added].

Reviewing Niall Ferguson's commissioned biography of Kissinger in 2015, in "Kissinger – Revered and reviled," Codevilla wrote:

> By the time Kissinger wrote, rational-choice theory, sometimes otherwise known as game theory, had bolstered the elite's visceral notion that nuclear war was just too, too much for anyone. Thomas Schelling, Kissinger's colleague down the hall at Harvard, had drawn up a matrix that shows that compromise is the best way for nations to maximize their achievement of conflicting goals. This, of course, assumes that the conflicting parties are interchangeable. Kissinger's work on international affairs is based on this assumption. It is a priori, abstract. Hence, in the Kantian tradition, it is "idealistic." By the same token, it is removed from reality.
>
> Indeed, that is the attractiveness of the Schelling-Kissinger approach to international affairs: it allows folks in positions of responsibility to imagine that numbers and kinds, and above all that functions of weapons do not matter, and that neither do the differences between the characters, ideas, or religions of peoples.

Codevilla was one of a handful of American strategists who foresaw the potential of missile defense and its capacity to break the Cold War deadlock, and his dismissal of Kissinger's dependence on game theory had the authority of the victor in the great debate over America's strategic direction in the late 1970s. All of Codevilla's reasons for abhorring Kissinger were true, and more. The reigning academic wisdom won over the American establishment: it taught that players with similar forces could only annihilate each other or reach a détente. They could harry each other with limited wars that did not reach the nuclear threshold. The establishment embraced this pseudo-scientific, mathematicized nuclear strategy and its policy mirages: flexible response, limited nuclear war, countervalue versus counterforce targeting, and strategic arms limitation. That misguided way of thinking drew the United States into the Vietnam morass, with dire consequences. Kissinger first promulgated the flawed theory that lured America into Vietnam, and then stage-managed our humiliating withdrawal.

Nonetheless, half a century after the Vietnam debacle, Henry Kissinger has become the elder statesman of American foreign policy, a voice of caution against utopian adventurism. "Henry Kissinger is a bastard," a senior statesman of one of America's Asian allies told me recently. "But he looks like a giant compared to the people who are running American foreign policy today. Kissinger is eminently sane, and they are crazy." If the definition of insanity is doing the same thing over and over again and expecting a different result, my interlocutor – who had dealt with Kissinger during the Indochina peace negotiations – was exactly correct. For all his missteps, Kissinger was one of the last redoubts of sanity in American foreign policy, cautioning against adventurism that might draw the United States into war with Russia or China.

The conduct of foreign policy remains a monopoly of the elites, and Kissinger, the ultimate elitist, was a statesman who warned us against overreach, in opposition to the utopian wing of the elite, e.g., neoconservatives like Victoria Nuland obsessed with regime change in Russia, or hawks like John Bolton and Mike Pompeo fixated on regime change in China. Codevilla's "country party" is not a major factor in foreign policy, except to the limited extent that it digs in its heels against excessive spending on the Ukraine war. The echo chamber of the mainstream media shields the country party from information that might disrupt the prevailing story that Russia is the new Nazi Germany, and politicians of both parties find it expedient to blame America's economic problems on China. In a June 2023 Gallup poll, Americans still favored support for Ukraine's attempt to reclaim all its territory from Russia by a margin of 62–33 percent, virtually unchanged from the year prior.

That would have disappointed Codevilla, who early on advocated the partition of Ukraine to forefend ethnic strife between the Ukrainian and Russophone elements of the population in a 2014 *Washington Times* article:

> Stalin drew the Ukrainian Soviet Socialist Republic's borders to place a strong minority of ethnic Russians into the same jurisdiction as ethnic Ukrainians. He did this to prevent a disruptively Ukrainian identity within the Soviet Union. If Ukraine ever tried to revolt, Moscow could always use strife between ethnic Ukrainians on the country's Western side and ethnic Russians on the Eastern end to bring it to heel. In fact, ever since Ukraine declared independence in 1991, Russia has fomented strife to try reabsorbing the country. Ukrainian-speaking Ukrainian Catholics want an independent Ukraine. Russian speaking Russian-Orthodox Ukrainians want one tied to Moscow. There is no reconciling the two.
>
> In short, saving Ukraine from its Stalinist legacy will have to mean splitting the country.

And he wrote in 2019 in "What's Russia to Us," with the notable subheading "Up from Russophobia":

> The US would be more secure geopolitically were Russia merely one of several European powers. But it has always been an empire, whose size has varied with time. An independent Ukraine has always been the greatest practical limitation on Russia's imperial ambitions. That is very much a US interest, but is beyond our capacity to secure...nothing should be geopolitically clearer than that the natural policy for both America and Russia is not to go looking for opportunities to get in each other's way.

The present military stalemate in Ukraine validates Codevilla's judgment that an independent Ukraine "is beyond our capacity to secure." Surely Codevilla, were he alive today, would advocate a quick armistice and a negotiated solution that assigned the Russophone districts of Eastern Ukraine to Russia. And he again would have been marginalized by an establishment that has closed ranks around a failed scheme for regime change in Russia.

Angelo Codevilla was able to embrace a cautious political rationalism that eschewed world-changing adventures, as well as a scientific optimism that envisioned a path out of the zero-sum game of geopolitics. He was both the learned translator of Machiavelli and the physics student drawn to the lodestar of Edward Teller. We could not educate a Codevilla today, nor find a Teller to inspire him if we did. The last fundamental discoveries in physics were published in the mid-1920s, just as Teller (born 1908) entered university, a time when – at least for physicists – to be young was very heaven.

The past fifty years have seen clever applications of quantum theory to computation and other technologies, but no fundamental progress. That has left scientific thinking in an extreme state of agnosticism. If you don't know where you are going, any road will get you there. Today's American scientific world resembles nothing more than the first-century genius Hero of Alexandria, who invented a steam engine but used it to make temple doors open as if by magic, and devised the first linear program but used it to automate a puppet show. The clever but feckless Greeks were crushed by the rougher and more practical Romans.

Physics has decayed into the indifferentism and relativism of multiverse theory, in which anything can happen. Our best scientific minds are profiled as undergraduates by Google and Microsoft and whisked down the memory holes of Big Tech. In Codevilla's generation, the best and brightest went to NASA. In 2018, thousands of Google employees protested the company's involvement in artificial-intelligence applications for satellite imaging for the

Defense Department, and Google terminated the program for fear of losing key talent.

The "country party" isn't enough. Codevilla envisioned a revolt against the elites and anticipated the rise of Donald Trump. Trump did not trouble to appoint a science advisor during the first three years of his administration, and his defense secretaries showed no interest in the cutting-edge physics that continued to preoccupy Codevilla until his death. As long as science remains the monopoly of the liberal elite, we will not be able to revive the scientific optimism that inspired Codevilla as a college student and led us to victory in the Cold War. But there is no conservative philosophy of science to speak of. Conservative political philosophy looks for unchanging truth, but there are no unchanging truths in science, which always strives to replace existing theories with better ones. In popular culture, the greatest achievements of 20th-century science and mathematics – Einstein's relativity, quantum theory, and Gödel's incompleteness theorems – are linked to the assertion that there is no absolute truth.

Angelo Codevilla's greatness lay in his ability to grasp this dilemma by both horns, to paraphrase Frank Meyer. But he was singularly great. To say that we shall not look upon his like again is not an encomium but a sad statement of fact.

If we wish to advance his program, we will have to do something different. We require a scientifically competent political elite, and we can best honor Codevilla's memory by considering how to cultivate it.

BRIAN T. KENNEDY

ANGELO CODEVILLA, COMMON SENSE, AND MISSILE DEFENSE

ANGELO CODEVILLA had a common refrain that the United States was not a serious country. It was not that the American people were not a serious people. They were. And they were also a good and moral people. They had demonstrated that in the Revolutionary War, the Civil War, two world wars, and the Cold War. It was, rather, that the American people had elected representatives and presidents who were manifestly unserious and had embraced a statecraft in the late 20th and early 21st century that bordered on suicidal. It was Codevilla's view that the continuance of such suicidal tendencies was unworthy of a free people.

A scholar and practitioner of national-security strategy, Codevilla was a great man and teacher who spent his life discerning exactly what kind of strategy and policies America should be pursuing in order to defend itself. It was his project to recover an American common sense when it came to national-security policy. He understood classical political philosophy, history, and the thought of the American founders with a precision that few other American thinkers possessed. The American common sense that he wrote about could be drawn from the words and deeds of George Washington, Alexander Hamilton, John Adams, and his son John Quincy Adams, to name but a few.

He was a master of the original America First brand of foreign policy. It asked the simple question: "What was good for America and the American people?" There was no secondary consideration.

In our past we were a commercial republic and had the interests of a commercial republic; we were not indifferent to what happened in the world because it was with the world that we would engage in commerce. We needed then to have an adequate naval capability in order to ensure that we could export our goods on the high seas. And in the modern age of warfare, where armies and navies could be transported over long distances, we needed military capabilities adequate to deter our enemies and, when necessary, to make war.

Codevilla believed Americans had an inadequate understanding of war and of the necessity for determining what it required. He wrote with Paul Seabury in *War: Ends and Means*: "knowledge of the necessary conditions for human freedom entails an appreciation of the nature of war because freedom can only be enjoyed by people ready, willing, and able to fight for it."

Codevilla believed we were living in a kind of "magic kingdom" where Americans no longer took seriously the meaning of war. Even after September 11, Codevilla believed that Americans misunderstood the nature of what we were fighting. We called Islam a religion of peace when it clearly was not. We created a security state within the United States – the TSA, the Department of Homeland Security, the Patriot Act, and the like – changing the way we lived *our* lives rather than seeking to punish and change the lives of those that had attacked us, namely the Wahhabists in Saudi Arabia. For Codevilla it was a cardinal sin that we would have our freedom abridged rather than taking whatever military or strategic actions were required to ensure that that was not necessary.

However politically expedient, it was a bad signal to the Islamic world – which believed itself at war with America and the West – to turn to Saudi Arabia immediately and accept them as a force of moderate Islam that would ostensibly check the more-radical elements throughout the Sunni world. As such, the Saudis paid no obvious price for allowing terrorists to be trained and equipped on their soil. Indeed, Codevilla argued in the pages of the *Claremont Review of Books* that it was inconceivable that the attacks on September 11 could have been pulled off without the assistance of Saudi intelligence.

That the United States did not punish Saudi Arabia was to fail to distinguish friends from enemies, and to prefer the path of making war on those elements of the Sunni world that were easiest to make war upon, namely Afghanistan and Iraq. However satisfying it may have been to go after the nation that for a time harbored Osama bin Laden and, in the case of Iraq, a nation with a Sunni leader in Saddam Hussein, it was unclear that we were deterring future terrorist attacks on the United States and the West.

Indeed, because we were not willing to take revenge on the immediate source of the problem, the Wahhabists, and to do so in a way that struck fear in not only the Saudis but also other sponsors of terrorism – such as Syria, Jordan, and the Palestine Liberation Organization – the "war on terror" appeared to be war for the sake of war.

That we would compound such poor decision-making with the wild idea of turning Iraq and, to a lesser extent, Afghanistan into democratic regimes signaled to the world that America was living in a kind of strategic fantasy, where the well-being of other nations was put before the well-being of our own. But for Codevilla, a war rightly waged was to establish a peace that conformed with the American way of life, which is to say, a republic that defended the human freedom of the American people. Operation Iraqi Freedom was not that – it was not for our good, as announced, but for liberation of the Iraqi people.

To put a finer point on it, however noble it may have been in theory to create democratic regimes in those nations, the people of Iraq and Afghanistan were ill-suited to become liberal democrats who respected the rights of man. Moreover, for Codevilla, it was not the duty of the United States to make them otherwise. And, when all was said and done, the US State Department created in those countries "democratic" regimes that adhered to a version of Islamic law antithetical to the very principles we were trying to defend.

As such, Codevilla saw in America's Global War on Terrorism a failure of basic strategy and common sense: we are spending the lives of our military men and women for the good of people in a faraway land rather than for the good of the American people.

This kind of thinking placed Codevilla far outside the academic world where he spent most of his life. Because he relied on the study of statesmanship, prudence, and common sense, he had no "theory of international relations." Theories were for academics who sought to darken rather than illuminate the path forward. If you were operating based on common sense, your approach was by definition not theoretical. The well-being of the American republic was at stake. This was not a theoretical matter.

This approach applied especially to his understanding of the US intelligence community and to his tenure on the professional staff of the Senate Intelligence Committee. In this role he became a scourge of the Central Intelligence Agency, calling them to account for failing to demonstrate even a modicum of competency when it came to the most basic of issues in the late 1970s and 1980s. He wrote in an essay in summer 1983 for the *Washington Quarterly*:

> In 1977 the country first learned that the Soviet Union's buildup of strategic weapons was rapidly achieving its objective: to provide the Soviet Union with the equipment to survive, fight, and win a nuclear war. It also learned that this equipment would be largely in place by about 1980, that the Soviets had been pursuing this capability since at least the mid-1960s, that the United States' intelligence agencies had had enough data to sound the warning. Instead, however, the National Intelligence Estimates (NIEs) had been telling policymakers that the Soviet Union would not undertake efforts that, in fact, it had

undertaken. In short, the estimators had missed a huge, ominous development unfolding before their very eyes.

In the fall of 1978 the country learned that, even as the Shah of Iran was being toppled from his throne by a movement openly organized in Paris, Washington, Beirut, Tehran, as well as in Baku, USSR, the CIA was estimating that Iran was not in a revolutionary or even in a prerevolutionary situation and that the shah would be an important part of Iranian politics into the foreseeable future.

These observations may not today seem earth-shattering. But at the time, with Codevilla on the professional staff of the Senate Intelligence Committee, they were. In a document declassified and approved for release in 2010, a memo to the deputy director of Central Intelligence, John McMahon, from August 24, 1983, John Bross suggested that a key CIA commission he was leading was likely to have little impact on the Senate so long as Codevilla remained on the staff. Codevilla, in other words, was not going to let the CIA, even during the Reagan administration, get away with the politicization of intelligence that may be essential for our national survival.

Whether it was the politicization of the National Intelligence Estimates, the CIA's full knowledge that the Soviet Union was engaging in a massive nuclear buildup, the mishandling of Soviet defectors, or the failures of counterintelligence that led to the Soviet penetration of the CIA, Codevilla saw that the intelligence community existed mostly above the reach of the political branches of government, which were unable to oversee operations effectively despite the efforts in the 1970s, not least of the Church Committee, to reign in their power. Although a certain degree of politicization was inevitable, the intelligence community's bureaucracy created a level of incompetence that to Codevilla was dangerous in the extreme. That he spoke publicly about such matters made him loved, hated, and feared.

It was during this period that Codevilla also focused on what would become one of President Reagan's chief strategic priorities: the building of a national missile defense. Called the Strategic Defense Initiative (SDI) and derided by Senator Ted Kennedy and the media as "Star Wars," it was Reagan and the Committee on the Present Danger's answer to both the Soviet nuclear buildup and the USSR's possession of a missile-defense system despite such systems' being limited by the 1972 ABM Treaty.

Codevilla chronicled his work and the debate surrounding SDI in his 1988 book *While Others Build: A Common Sense Approach to the Strategic Defense Initiative*. It was both a defense of President Reagan's ambition to protect the United States against Soviet ballistic missiles and an examination of the myriad arguments used against missile defense by its opponents, most especially those on the American Left – abetted by Soviet propagandists – who used specious technical and scientific arguments against the possibility of SDI succeeding.

As the book's title would suggest, it was a common-sense approach. Guided by the Aristotelian observation that everything is done for a purpose, Codevilla's strategic common sense was thus: Nations build a military capable of waging war. They do so for a purpose. The purpose is either to make war for a strategic end or to deter other nations from making war against them.

In the modern age, nations were not limited to armies with crossbows or cannons. In the modern age there was advanced artillery that could project lethal force from miles away. And there were air forces with fighter aircraft and long-range bombers. There were navies that could likewise launch artillery and missilery. Both from land and sea, ballistic missiles with nuclear warheads could be launched, enter space, and reenter thousands of miles away with precision.

These ballistic missiles can be decisive in a war. If used successfully against a nation, they could destroy the political administration such that it is unable to govern and might have to surrender to a foreign power. Not only could lives be lost in such devastation, but so too the constitutional control and territorial integrity of the nation.

For Codevilla, who took war seriously, these were not abstractions. He observed that in Washington, however, the "foreign policy class" cared far more about the ABM Treaty and its limitations on defense and outright ban of a "national" missile defense than they did the survival of the country. It should be noted that under the 1972 ABM Treaty both the Soviet Union and the United States were allowed to defend their nation's capital and an ICBM launch site to ensure both the continuation of government and the threat of mutually assured destruction.

In launching SDI, Reagan said on March 23, 1983:

> What if free people could live secure in the knowledge that their security did not rest upon the threat of instant US retaliation to deter a Soviet attack, that we could intercept and destroy strategic ballistic missiles before they reached our own soil or that of our allies?
>
> I know this is a formidable, technical task, one that may not be accomplished before the end of this century. Yet, current technology has attained a level of sophistication where it's reasonable for us to begin this effort. It will take years, probably decades of effort on many fronts. There will be failures and setbacks, just as there will be successes and breakthroughs. And as we proceed, we must remain constant in preserving the nuclear deterrent and maintaining a solid capability for flexible response. But isn't it worth every investment necessary to free the world from the threat of nuclear war? We know it is.

Like Reagan, Codevilla saw in the Soviet ballistic-missile buildup a design to wage war against and defeat the United States. If it were to remain a free country capable of its own defense, the United States would therefore require both offensive nuclear ballistic missiles and a ballistic-missile-defense system. We would need this because the Soviet Union had built and was improving its own missile capabilities.

In this debate the details mattered. If both sides were going to have nuclear weapons, and both constructed a strategic defense, then the number of missiles, the number of interceptors, and the effectiveness of both were critical. Codevilla points out in *While Others Build* that the Soviet Union had converted some three hundred counterforce missiles into a system with some six thousand counterforce warheads. This Soviet system used small nuclear warheads that would explode in proximity to an attacking US nuclear warhead. The Soviets did not busy themselves with perfection. However crude and whatever fallout there might be from using nuclear warheads to destroy nuclear warheads, the Soviet Union believed that was necessary strategically for them to win.

In a great paradox between the godless Communists of the Soviet Union and the God-fearing free people of the United States, it was the Soviet policy to destroy incoming nuclear warheads whereas it was, and is even to this day, the US policy to prefer instead the destruction of Soviet (now Russian) civilian populations. As Codevilla framed the American position, "Killing nuclear warheads bad! Killing people, good!" Reagan sought to change that dynamic. He believed it inherently the moral position to prevent a nuclear attack rather than retaliate to one. For Reagan and Codevilla it was simple common sense.

Even more, it was by no means certain that the US strategy of mutually assured destruction would prevail. That we have not engaged in nuclear war is not exactly the point. The North Koreans, the Chinese, the North Vietnamese, the Iranians, the Iraqis, and the Afghans have not appeared much fazed by our nuclear weapons. And the Soviet Union, who did take them seriously, made plans to counter them. Whether the United States would have achieved victory over the Soviet Union in open war is an ongoing debate. The Soviet Union had built, and Russia still possesses, a missile-defense system that could, it is estimated, protect 75 percent of its people. They may not have been able to defend the entirety of the Soviet Union, but they would have, if these numbers are right, been able to preserve their nation. Could the same have been said of the United States?

These were things analysts could study, military planners could make preparations for, and scientists and engineers could build. Codevilla became intimate with each piece of the puzzle. Could we build enough ballistic-missile interceptors, space-based interceptors, or space-based lasers so as to discourage the Soviet Union from using their nuclear arsenal against the United States? These were practical, real-world concerns that Codevilla had. These were problems that had to be solved in order to win the war that may someday come, and whose solutions could, at a minimum, deter an attack on the United States.

Despite the best efforts of Codevilla and President Reagan, the United States does not today have an effective national missile-defense system. We have a rudimentary system whose primary purpose is to stop a limited number of North Korean missiles aimed at the western United States. It cannot stop Russian or Chinese nuclear ballistic missiles. Nor can it stop a ship-launched ballistic missile from said countries or from Iran, nor the myriad advanced missiles, drones, and hypersonic-reentry vehicles such countries can produce. Today it would appear that our missile-defense systems are designed primarily to give the illusion to an otherwise uninformed public that we are defended.

This was the worst of all worlds for Codevilla. Not only was the United States not defended, but opponents of missile defense could claim in fact that one existed. The billions that have been put into research and some interceptor deployment in Alaska, in California, and aboard some Aegis cruisers have served as a kind of science project that promises annual progress toward building an effective system. But the US defense industry – making many billions more producing armaments for America's war in Iraq and Afghanistan and now Ukraine – is mostly indifferent to its overall success. The possibility that war might actually come to the

United States from Russia or China by ballistic-missile attack is simply unthinkable, and therefore missile defense became, and still is, a minor sideshow within America's defense establishment.

President Trump believed very much in missile defense during his first term, as Codevilla pointed out in his last book, *America's Rise and Fall Among Nations*. Trump even did the unthinkable by advocating a space-based layer of defense in the 2019 Missile Defense Review (MDR). But he was not able to reorient the defense establishment in such short order, and, in Codevilla's view, when the Biden administration came in it treated missile defense and Trump's Space Force as little more than an easily avoided bureaucratic nicety.

The failure to produce an effective missile defense revealed for Codevilla, yet again, the moral and intellectual corruption of America's military and political elites. If everything is done for a purpose, what was the purpose of leaving America undefended? Why should America be left to the tender mercies of its enemies when it came to the threat of ballistic-missile attack?

In his reasoning, the wise men of American statecraft had worked for nearly fifty years to ensure the United States was vulnerable to a nuclear attack, believing that vulnerability was somehow a virtue, that vulnerability would lead to a strategic stability where both sides would be afraid of using their weapons. Codevilla knew better. He understood that the Russians and the Chinese would work toward strategic dominance. Why would they not? And although nuclear war had not occurred between the United States and the Communist nations, it was not at all clear that they had the same reservations as the United States about the use of nuclear weapons in the future.

It is for this reason Codevilla wanted for America a robust offensive nuclear ballistic-missile arsenal and an effective national missile defense that could demonstrate to the Soviet Union or to Communist China America's determination to defend itself come what may. Codevilla feared that the failure to build a ballistic-missile-defense system – and today the atrophying of our offensive ballistic-missile capabilities – signaled instead confusion at best, and at worst, submission.

Indeed, it might suggest that the United States has embraced a kind of nihilism whereby our national survival is no longer a primary concern of American policymakers, who instead live in a kind of death cult that refuses to accept that war may come to these United States from enemies who wish for our destruction – or in any event that nuclear ballistic missiles, the most awesome weapons ever invented, were somehow without strategic importance.

Codevilla highlighted these problems especially regarding our posture towards China. Since its inception in 1949, the People's Republic of China, a Communist nation, has seen the United States as an enemy to its revolution. But Chinese strategy has been to prepare for battle that would not be advantageous to the United States, namely in the South China Sea.

Communist China possesses a first-rate nuclear arsenal with hypersonic-reentry vehicles and supersonic cruise missiles that would present a very lethal problem for the US Navy operating in the Pacific. Such weapons are likely to keep us out of conflict with them lest we lose, for instance, an American aircraft carrier. The psychological effects of such a loss would be devastating to the United States.

And so, it is more than likely we would be restrained in our use of military force to defend Taiwan. Even the resupply of Taiwan, should the People's Liberation Army Navy blockade the island, may prove too dangerous since the logical outcome would be direct confrontation between the US Navy and the PLA Navy. Taking the necessary steps to reinforce Taiwan, Codevilla believed, was therefore much to be desired since that kind of practical deployments of offensive and defensive weapons systems would signal to the PRC that America was prepared to defend its interests throughout the Pacific. However patient Communist China was in achieving its strategic objectives, America's withdrawal from the Pacific would only whet their appetite.

Codevilla knew that when war comes – if Communist China

makes that decision – it will be total war, and there will not be many options available to the United States. The PRC is well aware of the United States' strategic shortcomings. And the Chinese know that American military planners have not prepared – in any serious way – for war against them. Make no mistake: the Chinese have prepared for this. They have on multiple occasions had large-scale civil-defense exercises where they moved significant parts of their population into underground shelters. They have signaled they are prepared to fight a nuclear war.

Not only does China maintain advanced nuclear weaponry with the readiness and public resolve to deploy it, they possess excellent anti-satellite technology and are hard at work on their own missile defenses. They are also far advanced with their space program, demonstrated by their landing of a spacecraft on the far side of the moon. Codevilla pointed out that in doing so, the Chinese were signaling that they could do *anything* that the United States could do when it came to space. Moreover, since US offensive capabilities, whether by missiles or conventional forces, require the use of satellites, the PRC's potential to limit or negate the effectiveness of the United States by use of anti-satellite weapons was clear.

In all these failures of policy and statecraft, especially regarding Communist China, Codevilla saw not only a lack of seriousness, but even self-deception bordering on delusion. These could be remedied only by recovering an older, common-sense understanding of American statesmanship. Even after a lifetime witnessing such failures, Codevilla had not grown cynical; he believed in the genius of the American people and their capacity to get things right, no matter the corruption of their elected representatives. This was due, in small part, to his simple belief in the American experiment and God's blessing on his almost-chosen people.

Among God's blessings was, of course, the scholar and teacher Angelo Codevilla, who not merely helped point the United States in the right direction but, with love, affection, and a hard patriotism, also made those around him better in the process.

THOMAS CODEVILLA AND BRIAN T. KENNEDY

IN MEMORY OF ANGELO MARIA CODEVILLA (1943–2021)

These remarks were given at a memorial for friends and family at Andis Wines in Plymouth, California, on October 20, 2021.

THOMAS CODEVILLA

WELCOME, FRIENDS, family, community members, and policy nerds. I'm Thomas Codevilla, Angelo's youngest son. Thank you all for coming.

We're here today because, after years of gently suggesting that Dad get more rest, the good Lord took matters into his own hands.

Dad was many things to many people; it is natural to ask at a memorial, "Who was he really?" I will not speak on his intellectual legacy. People with actual doctorates are here to do that. To the extent it may help, though, here's how I understood him.

Imagine, if you will, being born poor into World War II Italy with a predeceased father. You steal fruit from orchards to keep your belly full; your scalp bears a hatchet scar from a fight with a preteen Communist gang. You bathe in a cauldron. You are first in your class every year because you have to be. Standing at your father's grave, your mother lectures you on duty and family.

After your unscrupulous Argentinian tango-violinist relatives steal the money your mother sent ahead, you only have enough money for the boat ride to America. You experience running hot water for the first time on that boat, and the gratitude never leaves you. Every August 8 for the rest of your life, you celebrate the anniversary of your disembarkation.

You learn English from John Wayne movies and perfect your accent by repeating Winston cigarette ads. You deliver newspapers to mobsters; you learn to knife fight to protect yourself at school; you build amateur rockets and gleefully shoot them over the Hudson River into New York. You meet your future wife by walking straight into a Valentine's Day mixer *to which you were not invited*, asking her, "Good evening miss, would you like to twist?" and then taking her out for her first beer at age eighteen.

Now ask yourself, given that early life, what room is there in you for fear or self-doubt? When you have realized your wildest dreams through will and self-reliance, why stop dancing with the one that brought you?

Dad's mindset created some obstacles and demolished others. When he was in the navy, one of his officer tests consisted of managing a simulated crisis on a ship; after three frenzied minutes of his trying to complete every task himself, his commanding officer stopped him and told him that the point of the exercise was delegation. Dad liked the story more than the moral.

His informal motto was *make them stop you*. If there wasn't a fence or a federal injunction, or even if there was and he didn't think it was "serious," he'd go ahead with what he thought was right and make the powers that be pipe up if they had any grief.

On the flip side, I once found myself with him on horseback, stuck on the top of a hill at midnight, a freshly killed elk in our panniers and wolves howling in the trees, scared out of my mind. I saw no way off the hill. Dad calmly dismounted, used a rock to demolish a fence panel, and leaned back in the saddle, as one would in a La-Z-Boy, as our horses picked their way down the hill.

On one horse-pack trip deep in the backcountry, a kid in our group got the flu as we started the three-day ride out to the cabin. On top of a mountain pass in a sideways hailstorm, a cinch on the sick kid's horse came loose and she toppled off, then commenced to get sick. I swear, on my life, I saw Dad smile and hum some cheery little tune to himself as he calmed the horse and reattached the saddle.

When a bear ate almost all our food in the middle of another pack trip, that, to Dad, was a blessed opportunity to fish more for our dinner.

It's old news, but he suffered no fools. I bet his former students will hear his refrain "Get serious" in their dreams. While I was in law school, I finally asked him to define his terms: what does "Get serious" mean? Out came the old saw that those who are serious about the ends should be serious about the means. I replied that he was begging the question. He replied instantly that to be serious was to prepare and believe so thoroughly that one could stand in front of the whole world, maybe even God, and speak the Truth, with a capital T. How are you going to argue with a guy who imagines haranguing the Almighty every time he talks?

He walked that walk; I have yet to hear of anyone else who went through two heart transplants with total continuity of attitude.

My favorite story was when Dad apparently dressed down a two-star general in a meeting, ruining any chance of getting the general's support for his pet project. Roy Godson took Dad aside afterwards and asked, in as many words, what the hell he thought he was doing. "The guy is a schmuck," Dad said. Roy replied, "And who are you, the unschmucker?"

Everyone who knew him should be nodding right now. Dad unschmucked all day and twice on Sundays. Dad would, and frequently did, unschmuck for free.

He put Solzhenitsyn's *Gulag Archipelago* in my hands at age twelve, then asked me for a book report on it. He showed me a passage of Solzhenitsyn's that made him do that crazy-eyed half-smile, half-snarl thing he only did when he was really fired up.

> Violence has nothing to cover itself with but lies, and lies can only persist through violence. And it is not every day and not on every shoulder that violence brings down its

> heavy hand: It demands of us only a submission to lies, a daily participation in deceit – and this suffices as our fealty.
>
> And therein we find, neglected by us, the simplest, the most accessible key to our liberation: a *personal nonparticipation in lies!* Even if all is covered by lies, even if all is under their rule, let us resist in the smallest way: Let their rule hold *not through me!*

Parallels to current events aside, that is how I understood my dad.

I still wish he had slowed down more to enjoy what he had built, but that was not Dad. So please, before you get back to your lives and your work, *pause* and consider how many walks of life this crowd represents, how one man could live enough lives to assemble all of you.

If you want to honor him, I have two suggestions. First, drink this wine made from the grapes he grew and share stories with someone from another life of his; the intelligence officer in him would appreciate a final, thorough debrief. Thank God for whatever experience brought you here today.

Then wake up tomorrow and work a little harder – because Dad's got the day off.

BRIAN T. KENNEDY

THANK YOU EVERYONE for joining us to honor and remember Angelo Codevilla.

For his family, let me say that there was never a conversation I had with him in which it was not clear that whatever Angelo was doing, it was in the service of his family and his country. He was extremely proud of his family and the life he had built and lived so passionately here in America.

I, like many of you, knew Angelo through his writings before I ever met the man. Knowing what I do about Angelo, one might say that his writings form a kind of love letter to his adopted country. I hope for this tribute to be a kind of love letter to him and to his family.

I was talking to one of the Claremont Institute's founders and one of Angelo's friends, in the days after Angelo passed. Chris Flannery had just done a podcast on the greatness of America and the Statue of Liberty. Afterwards Angelo emailed Chris Flannery the following:

> On the foggy morning of August 8, 1955, it was my privilege to stand on the port rail of the American Export Lines SS *Constitution*, along with every other emigrant on board, as the ship slipped past the Statue and into NY harbor, Pier 40. Nobody made a sound. All were overwhelmed. The only sounds I heard that morning were quiet sobs. Enormous satisfaction and anticipation. None of us really knew what awaited us. But everybody was awed and delighted that, finally, we were here! Countless prayers fulfilled.

One got the impression from Angelo that not long after arriving in New York, he thought, "What a beautiful place. I must defend it. These people don't seem to know how to do this. I need to teach them." Angelo Codevilla was a professor of international relations. That is a profession known for theories of international relations that range from realpolitik to isolationism and a slew of political variations on the theme, from neoconservativism to globalism to what is called, today, America Firstism.

Angelo Codevilla was none of these. He was a philosopher. One did not need a theory of international relations if he were guided by common sense and intelligence – not the kind that is produced in Langley, Virginia, but the kind that is between your ears. If you didn't have that, you needed more of it. If that were not possible, you were in deep trouble. For nearly all his professional career, Angelo believed we Americans were in deep trouble.

He was an early advocate of national missile defense based on the rather simple premise that if another nation has nuclear weapons that can and are intended to destroy you, it is only common sense that you have a defensive system to make sure that did not happen.

One of his finest books was *While Others Build*, which describes the debate in the 1980s over missile defense. He saw then just how unserious the nation was about matters critical to our national survival. He meant to change that. After September 11, all of Angelo's training and scholarship came into sharp focus as he emerged as the most serious and insightful analyst of why we were attacked and what must be done to ensure that it would never happen again. Here his common sense was melded with an unparalleled understanding of international affairs in a book called *No Victory, No Peace*. For Angelo the threefold question was rather basic: who did it, why did they do it, and what should our response be? This is rather straightforward and uncomplicated. The *who* of September 11 was not, in Angelo's estimation, the people of Afghanistan. Yes, the Afghans were harboring bin Laden, but their strategic thinking did not really extend much further than whether they were going to get paid to harbor the leader of al-Qaeda. For Angelo, the common-sense analysis was that fifteen of the nineteen hijackers were Saudi nationals and could not have pulled off the attack without the assistance and tacit support of the Saudi intelligence services – and therefore the Saudi government, and by extension the Saudi royal family.

The *why* was that they were sympathetic to a sect of Islamic teaching that believed in waging war on the infidel, namely us. When it came to *what* to do about it, for Angelo, the common-sense assessment was that there are five thousand members of the Saudi royal family. Some of them should hang or face murder charges for what they allowed to happen. That would send a signal to the Saudi royal family, and to tyrants throughout the world, that if you harbor al-Qaeda you will pay a heavy price. Indeed, you will pay with your life. Despots throughout the Middle East would have an immediate interest in making sure that any member of al-Qaeda would be turned over to the United States for justice to be served.

To Angelo's way of thinking, the fact that the US government did not hold Saudi Arabia to account, indeed covered for them at nearly every turn, also sent a signal – that the United States, because of its long ties to the Saudi royal family, could be bought off, financially, politically, and diplomatically. For all the tough talk about justice, we sent a signal to the world that we were not going to hold Saudi Arabia to account and, indeed, were going to let them get away with it. We were going to let corners of Saudi intelligence go on operating as they had before. Yes, Saudi Arabia may have become an ally in the war on terror, but the basic lie had been told, which everyone understood to be a lie, that we were not going to hold the perpetrators to account. We were going to hold someone else to account and see whether or not the American people could be mollified by such action.

This did not mean of course that there weren't people worthy of retribution for their part in Afghanistan or Iraq or Iran or elsewhere. But that war was not going to be waged against the main perpetrator, Saudi Arabia. Military actions were going to be had in Afghanistan and Iraq to massage domestic political concerns and achieve some unknown objective. This lie was so transparent, Angelo believed, it would implicate everyone within the American national-security establishment involved in the falsehood. That not only sent the wrong signal to the Islamic world, but it would also fundamentally alter the relationship of the US government and the national-security apparatus to the American people. This was itself the most damning thing, for the purpose of war is always to make your country better off.

For Angelo this was something so commonsensical that it should not even need to be articulated. It was a favorite phrase of Angelo's to say that this was not a serious country, or that this politician or another was not a serious man. Of course, he meant that it was deadly serious that we as a nation should have leaders who were going to defend America from all enemies, foreign and domestic.

As an aside, it was not long after Angelo had written these articles on September 11 for the *Claremont Review of Books* that he was teaching in one of our fellowship programs in Newport Beach. As it happened, we were staying at the Island Hotel, which had become a favorite place for the Saudi royal family to summer. For about five years straight, 75 percent of the hotel was occupied by the Saudis during the summer. On this occasion Angelo had arrived at his appointed time but had been given the wrong room number for the hospitality suite where we were meeting. He had been sent to the presidential suite, where senior members of the Saudi royal family were having a cocktail party of their own. It did not take long for Angelo to realize he was in the wrong place, and thankfully and even more importantly these Saudis didn't know what Angelo Codevilla looked like. Later it was reported to me that Angelo had to be restrained from making good on his policy of punishing the Saudi royal family for September 11. That was the Angelo we knew and loved.

Angelo saw things that others did not see. He diagnosed early that a populist rebellion was going on in American society between the people – what he called the country class – and those in Washington who thought themselves their betters, whom Angelo termed the ruling class. The main evangelist of his thesis was Rush Limbaugh, a populist himself, who found in Angelo's writing an intellectual expression of populism that could be understood in conservative political terms. At the heart of Angelo's criticism of the ruling class was the very American sensibility of "Who in the hell do they think they are?" That was always on his mind. Who in the hell were these people in Washington, DC, to govern us this way? He would document near the end of his life how America had become an oligarchy, and that there was much work to be done to recover American freedom. All of us believed Angelo would be with us to show us the way.

In reading his official obituary, people will find it said that he was on his third heart. I knew him when he was on his first heart. I had visited him at Stanford University where doctors had assessed that he had an enlarged heart that was going to fail him. It would be nothing short of a miracle to find a heart that would be compatible, as all heart transplants are. Angelo had asked me to come to him in part to see if I would serve as his literary executor. I agreed immediately, not fully even knowing the scope of the work, but assuming it meant making sure that any outstanding manuscripts get produced and that older books in print remain in print. It was easy to agree of course, not merely because such a thing would be good to do, but because the force of nature that was Angelo Codevilla could certainly not die. There were too many essays to produce, too many books to be written, too many lectures to be given.

A few weeks later I was in New York and Angelo called me. A young man in Utah had taken his own life and a heart therefore had been found. He asked if I could say a prayer for him that everything would go well with the transplant. So, from the tragedy of one man's life ending, Angelo's would continue. There was not a single interaction I had with Angelo that was not both humbling and exhilarating. Whether it was an essay, lecture, or phone call, you realized how much more there was to learn and how great a man Angelo was. And indeed, Angelo will always be known as a teacher. Not just from what he did in the classroom, not just from his books and essays, but for how he lived his life. He was a moral man who expressed a loving devotion for his wife Anne and love, affection, and pride in his children. His was an example of a life well led.

Angelo Codevilla knew how the world worked. He believed it his mission to teach his countrymen all that he knew. He wanted them to live as free men and women. In these dark times of ours, I have been reading a lot about angels and demons and God's intercessions. In so many ways, the aptly named Angelo Maria Codevilla has been one of America's guardian angels. I pray that all the lives he has touched will take to heart and mind the many lessons he was trying to teach us. And I pray that he rests in peace knowing all the good he has done for so many of his countrymen.

ACKNOWLEDGMENTS

I would like to recognize the generous support of the Neal & Jane Freeman Foundation. Without their kind contribution, neither our 2023 event honoring Angelo in Washington, DC, nor this book would have been possible.

Editing a book is no easy feat, and so I would also like to extend thanks to the duo we call at Claremont the "Brothers Gannon." Jake and Ryan, thank you both for your diligent labor in putting this volume together.

Ryan P. Williams

CONTRIBUTORS

THOMAS CODEVILLA is one of Angelo Codevilla's sons and a Claremont Institute Publius fellow.

DAVID CORBIN is Emeritus Professor of Politics at Providence Christian College. Dr. Corbin has previously taught political philosophy, American politics, international relations, and politics and literature at the University of New Hampshire, Boston University, and The King's College over two decades.

DAVID P. GOLDMAN is a Washington fellow of the Claremont Institute with a focus on China, American manufacturing, and trade policy. He is concurrently Deputy Editor of *Asia Times* and a senior writer for *Law & Liberty*.

STEVEN F. HAYWARD is the Edward L. Gaylord Visiting Professor of Public Policy at Pepperdine University. Dr. Hayward is a Senior Fellow at the Claremont Institute and was previously a Senior Resident Scholar at UC Berkeley's Institute of Governmental Studies..

BRIAN T. KENNEDY is a senior fellow, board member, and former president of the Claremont Institute. He is president of the American Strategy Group.

ROBERT REILLY is Director of the Westminster Institute and the author, most recently, of *America on Trial: A Defense of the Founding.*

J. MICHAEL WALLER is President of Georgetown Research and Senior Strategy Analyst for the Center for Security Policy.

RYAN P. WILLIAMS is President of the Claremont Institute and Publisher of the *Claremont Review of Books* and The American Mind.

INDEX

Note: Entries for "America" and "Codevilla, Angelo" have been omitted, as it may be presumed that every topic listed below relates to one or the other (and often both). For the sake of brevity, "AC" is used as shorthand for "Angelo Codevilla."

INDEX

A NOTE ON THE TYPE

FIGHTING ENEMIES FOREIGN AND DOMESTIC has been set in Fernando Mello's Brabo types, which he first developed during a typographic workshop at the Plantin-Moretus Museum in Antwerp and named in honor of Silvius Brabo, the mythic Roman savior of the ancient port city. As legend has it, Brabo defeated the giant Druon Antigoon, who terrorized the city by extorting taxes on shipping and demanding payment to cross the bridge over the river Scheldt, cutting off the hands of those who refused to pay. Brabo defeated the giant and paid him back in kind, tossing his severed hand into the Scheldt, an act that (so the story goes) is commemorated in the the city's name: the Dutch for "hand-throw" is hand werpen, *hence, Antwerpen. ❧ A distinctly modern type, Brabo acknowledges the proportions and crisp drawing of sixteenth-century faces like Garamond and Plantin, making it a fine choice for literary texts.*

DESIGN & COMPOSITION BY CARL W. SCARBROUGH